78

W9-CMB-142

SURVIVORS OF THE STONE AGE

SURVIVORS OF THE STONE AGE:

Nine Tribes Today

by REBECCA B. MARCUS

Illustrated with photographs

HASTINGS HOUSE PUBLISHERS

New York 10016

LIBRARY OF CONGRESS CATALOGING IN PUBLICATION DATA

Marcus, Rebecca B
    Survivors of the stone age.

    Bibliography: p.
    Includes index.
    SUMMARY: Describes the daily life, homes, and customs of nine tribes still living under Stone Age conditions in various areas of the world.
    1. Ethnology—Juvenile literature. [1. Ethnology] I. Title.
GN330.M36   301.2   75-6843
ISBN 0-8038-6726-3

Published simultaneously in Canada by
Saunders of Toronto, Ltd., Don Mills, Ontario

Printed in the United States of America

Contents

The Pygmies
Ituri Forest
Zaire

The Jivaro
Ecuador

The Kranhacarores
Xingu Preserve
Brazil

Bushmen
Kalahari Desert
Botswana

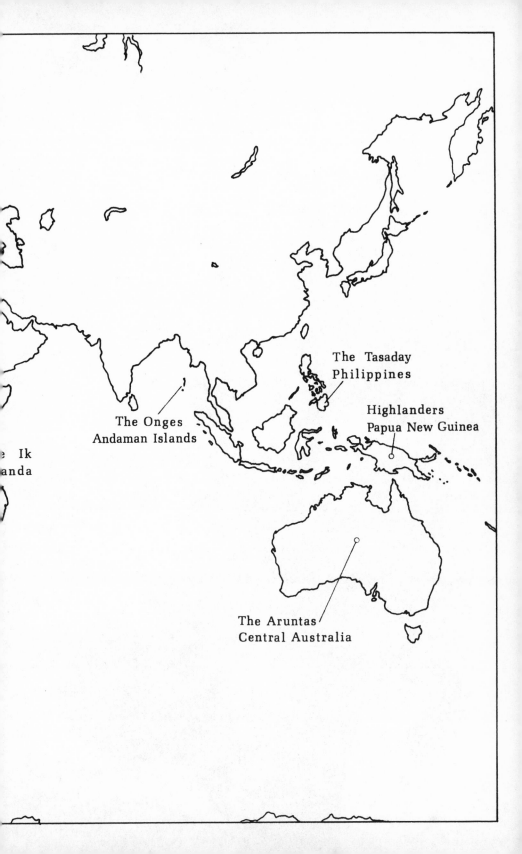

The Tasaday
Philippines

Highlanders
Papua New Guinea

The Onges
Andaman Islands

e Ik
anda

The Aruntas
Central Australia

Introduction

Stone Age Man, Past and Present

S TONE AGE MAN does not belong to any particular time or place. There are Stone Age people living now, in the Space Age, when men have walked on the moon. There are groups of Stone Age people living in South America, Africa, Asia, Australia and on islands in the Pacific and Indian Oceans. A very few remote Eskimos in North America are still Stone Age men.

What does it mean to say that certain people are still living in the Stone Age?

It means, simply, that they make their tools from stone, bone and wood instead of metal. They may use metal tools given them by others, but they have not learned how to make them. Of course, most men and women in our modern world would be unable to recognize iron ore, smelt out the metal and fashion it into tools, but the knowledge of this process is a part of our society and there are those who know how to apply it for the others.

When humans first appeared on the earth, probably about three million years ago, their first tools were wood, rocks and animal bones. By fastening a sharpened stone to a wooden handle, they made an ax, a spear, or an arrow. They got their food by gathering wild plants, fruits and seeds and by hunting with these stone weapons.

Thousands of generations later, people discovered how to plant and harvest crops. They learned that they could herd certain animals and raise them for food instead of depending entirely upon hunting for meat. Yet, seeds were still planted with sharpened sticks and ground was cleared with stone tools. Animals were butchered, skinned and cut with stone implements.

During man's early time on earth, he discovered how to make fire. Probably at first people saw a tree that had been struck by lightning and was burning. Realizing its use in frightening animals away from their encampments, they kindled sticks from the blazing tree and made their own fires from the already existing one. They then realized that they could make fire for themselves either by striking two stones together or rubbing two pieces of wood together hard and igniting dried grass with the resulting sparks.

About five thousand years ago, some men discovered that when two certain kinds of rock became very hot, thick liquids oozed out of them. When mixed together and then cooled, the hot liquids—copper and tin—became bronze. They found that bronze was a hard material that held a sharp edge better than stone.

More important, the hot mixture could be poured into molds and thus made into tools of many more shapes and sizes than stone. The people who began to use bronze tools had stepped out of the Stone Age into the Bronze Age.

An even greater improvement was made in tools when iron was later discovered. The hard metal could be beaten into the desired shape when it was cold, but better yet, when glowing hot it could be bent, twisted and hammered into almost any form with the use of proper tools. From there on, improvements in working iron and in adding small amounts of other metals to it when it was molten finally led to modern iron and steel machinery.

Yet in some parts of the world, far removed from trade routes on land and sea, there are still people who have never left the Stone Age.

We have learned much about Stone Age people by studying how the few present-day Stone Age groups live. By going to live among them, mastering their language, and gaining their trust, anthropologists have been able to give us a good picture of Stone Age man and his life.

Ever since man emerged on earth, people have found ways to make themselves comfortable in the environment in which they live and to try to understand it. How they do this, what tools and products they use, their language, religion, art, family life and social customs are all part of their way of life. It is their culture. A special branch of anthropology is called ethnology: this is the study of the culture of both ancient and modern people.

Anthropologists may study the living habits of New Yorkers of Italian parentage, or the blacks who emigrated from the West Indies to London. Often they go off to hard-to-reach places where there are people whose culture is very different from their own.

Many anthropologists are especially interested in studying today's Stone Age people. Since our remote ancestors lived mostly as these people now do, the scientists hope to learn how our own culture developed into what it is today.

Modern anthropologists sometimes live for years among the group they wish to study. They fill many notebooks with their observations, take thousands of photographs and reels of motion pictures, and record their questions and the answers, the sounds in a village, the music and singing, on tape. The reports they bring back give a vivid picture of the life of the people.

The results of their work point out a most important fact—all human beings, in spite of the differences in their cultures, have basically the same social needs. Every group, from Stone Age tribes living in jungles to our technological civilization, needs a set code of behavior toward its own members. All expect a certain kind of conduct between children and parents, husbands and wives, old people and the rest of its members, and toward persons in authority. All have customs that are intended to keep the group together as a whole; all have some way of expressing their awe of nature and what they consider the mysteries of the universe. Almost every group has some legend, explanation or belief of how they came to be on earth and what happens to a person's spirit when he dies.

Anthropologists stress that we must not use our own standards to judge other cultures. We must understand what is important to other people, their ideas and hopes, and their own wishes for their future. An African tribe's culture is different from that of a South

American Indian's or a European's, but that does not make one better than the other. The important thing is that a culture suits the people in the environment in which they live.

The nine tribes described in this book, have adapted to different kinds of environments. Some, the Andaman Islanders, live in steaming coastal jungles; others, the Pygmies, in deep forests; still others, the Kalahari Bushmen and the Arunta of Australia, live in desert areas. The Highlanders of New Guinea inhabit a pleasant land of steep mountains and the Tasaday make their homes along a rushing stream.

The customs of many of these tribes contrast in interesting ways. For example, the Tasaday and the Pygmies are particularly tender toward their children and encourage them to play. But the Jivaro frown upon any play, idleness, or laughter on the part of their children. Yet tribes that are geographically distant without contact with each other have developed some similar customs.

What is the future for Stone Age tribes, as they come into contact with modern ideas and machines? Anthropologists and many others ask this question but have no ready answer to it.

If a tribe substitutes most of a new culture for its old one, it usually becomes lost as a separate group. This has happened in New Zealand, where the Maoris, Stone Age people about a hundred years ago, have become so assimilated into the New Zealand culture that their own culture has almost disappeared.

Many primitive tribes have "disappeared" less gradually. Some were wiped out almost completely by disease. They had never been exposed to certain diseases of civilization such as smallpox, respiratory disorders, measles, and influenza, and therefore had no resistance to them. In the Caribbean Islands, for example, masses of Carib Indians fell ill and died after contact with explorers.

Stone Age people also have no defense against modern weapons. The Carib Indians who managed to escape disease perished by gunfire when the Europeans wanted their land.

Stone Age tribes today suffer most when people of technological cultures push into their territory in search for farm and ranch lands, oil, timber and other natural resources. Clashes between the two cultures are bound to take place. One group wants to keep its land, the other to exploit it. The group without technology is forced to give way to the one that has guns, bulldozers and heavy rock-breaking machinery.

It becomes the responsibility of a government to protect the primitive tribes living within its borders from being destroyed. But governments also think it necessary to protect the interests of the businessmen who invest in projects that destroy tribal habitats. In fact, some of the projects, like road-building, are the government's own.

The Ik, a Stone Age tribe of Africa, are a tragic illustration of what may happen to a group of people who have been forced into a strange environment that cannot support and sustain them and whose culture has therefore broken down completely. There seems to be no hope for the future survival of this tribe.

Anthropologists and others interested in Stone Age cultures, are strongly urging government agencies to curb the cruelty and greed of those taking over tribal lands. They have had some positive results in the Philippines, but few in South America, especially in Brazil. Some Indian tribes of the Brazilian jungle have been wiped out altogether and some, stripped of their hunting grounds, have become beggars. The future for the survival of many South American Indians, like the Kranhacarores, looks grim at the present time.

It is almost impossible in this Space Age for a tribe, once discovered by Western civilization, to remain untouched by it. In some few cases, outside influences are not as strong. Some tribes have found it possible to maintain their own way of life while adopting certain tools of western culture. For example, Pygmies who work for farmers may bring matches back into the forest upon their return home. When these are used up, however, they go back to their age-old way of making fire, carrying glowing coals from one encampment to another. A New Guinea tribesman, during a special ceremony, may stand almost naked, his body brightly painted, sporting a traditional headdress of wild bird feathers—and wearing a pair of sneakers to protect his feet. And yet these tribesmen of New Guinea were discovered only in the 1930's.

There are probably some more undiscovered Stone Age tribes in remote regions still living as their ancestors did thousands of years ago. Before a reader finishes this book, there may be a news report of another Stone Age tribe, just discovered in some hidden corner of the world.

1

The
Cave People of the Philippines
The Tasaday

A FTER LESS THAN half an hour's ride from the small city of Surallah in the Philippines, a helicopter landed in the rain forest of Mindanao on June 7, 1971. Out stepped a Filippino right into the Stone Age. He had come to make contact with the Tasaday people who, he had heard, lived in caves in this wild, almost unexplored mountainous country. From them he hoped to learn at first hand how Stone Age man lived.

The newcomer, Manuel Elizalde, was the head of PAN-AMIN—the Philippine Association for National Minorities, a government sponsored group. As its chief, he had been seeking out small tribes believed to be living isolated in the rain forest. He wanted to find them and get them government protection before they would be wiped out by greedy lumbermen who were pushing further into the forest. Acting on information he had received from a Filippino of another forest tribe, he succeeded in locating the Tasaday.

When the PANAMIN helicopter landed, one tense, frightened member of the tribe stepped out of the forest to greet Elizalde. The man had come to see if the newcomer had arrived to fulfil a prophecy handed down from father to son for hundreds of years. It foretold that if the Tasaday stayed together in their ancestral place, a bringer of great good would eventually appear.

Gradually, Elizalde gained the man's confidence and of the others who soon came to see the stranger who had dropped from the sky. But although during several visits to the forest they told him much about their mode of living, it was eight months before they felt secure enough to invite him to their settlement.

The name "Tasaday" means "People of the Caves," in the language of the neighboring Filippino tribes. And this is indeed what Elizalde saw in 1971—27 people living in three big limestone caves and a few smaller ones, in a cliff overlooking a rushing stream.

Dense forest growth hides the Tasaday settlement so well that it is invisible from the air, and sometimes even from a few yards away. There are no roads in this part of the forest, no way to reach the settlement from the outside, except by helicopter. The Tasaday have been living in the caves in the forest for possibly a thousand years, remote from other groups.

How the Tasaday first came to this forest no one knows, but they are certainly native Filippinos. Like them, they have brown skin, high cheekbones, and dark, curly hair, and are of slight build.

Tasaday women wear very short skirts made of orchid leaves and vines. The men wear only a loin cloth held by a thin string of vines, and the children are completely naked. The only decoration men and women use are three or four big, slender fiber loops hanging from their ears.

The Tasaday have no chief or leader, and they need none. They share their food, just as they share their few tools. They compete with no one, for they live in peace and harmony with each other. They are gentle, non-aggressive people, with no words in their language for anger, war, weapons, or hostility. Voices are never raised in anger or dispute.

Children are shown constant affection, and are never struck. The older ones help take care of the younger ones, play with them, show them how to slide down hills on banana leaves and how to catch tadpoles and crabs with their bare hands. They wash the little ones with the wood pulp the Tasaday use as soap. They carry them about on their shoulders as they wade in the streams, laughing as the tots pull their hair playfully.

A Tasaday family in the shelter of their cave.

A family is made up of a man, his wife, and their children. In some families a widowed mother or father stays with a son or daughter, and then there are three generations living together in their part of a cave. Each family collects its own firewood and does its own cooking. But a child feels free to wander over to another family and eat with them if he is hungry and his own meal is not ready.

There is plenty of food to be found in the forest, so there is no need to store or grow any. The Tasaday dig up wild yams which is their main food, bananas, palm leaf buds, ginger, berries, and other forest plants. Crabs, tadpoles, frogs, and small fish that they catch with their bare hands are special delicacies. Those that they do not eat as soon as caught, they wrap in a leaf twisted into a cone and bring back to their family.

A chance meeting in 1966 with a man from another tribe brought a few but important changes in the lives of the Tasaday.

Until then, a rock from the river, bound with a vine to a piece of wood for a handle, became a hammer. A scraper, used among other things to sharpen bamboo strips into knives, was made from a piece of stone ground to a sharp edge. For combs, most Tasaday still use flat pieces of bamboo and for dishes and pots, leaves or lengths of hollowed bamboo.

The Tasaday make fire with a fire drill. The firemaker sits on the ground or squats, and with his feet holds down a flat piece of wood with a small hole in it. Under the hole he puts some dried moss or leaves as tinder. Then, with his hands, he rotates a stick inside the hole. The friction of the stick against the sides of the hole causes enough heat to kindle sparks in the tinder. Carefully, he blows on the sparks and adds fuel to make the fire bigger.

The man who first brought changes into their lives was Dafal, a trapper from the Blit tribe, who live a little more than a day's foot-journey away. The Blit culture is more advanced than that of the Tasaday because they have sought contact with the outside world. The people use iron tools, live in thatched huts, raise cattle, and plant some crops.

One day Dafal went deeper into the rain forest than usual to set his traps. Suddenly he stumbled upon two almost-naked men who, terrified at the sight of a stranger dressed in clothing they had never seen, started to flee. Dafal called out not to be afraid, he would not harm them. The men seemed to understand and haltingly came toward him. They managed to communicate, for their two languages were quite similar.

Once they felt at ease, they became curious about his iron knife, his animal traps, and his clothing. Dafal, in turn, was curious about people who had never seen such things before. At his suggestion, the two Tasaday took Dafal to their settlement.

After seeing where they lived, he understood why, although his own tribe was not too far away, no one had known about the Tasaday. They never had to go more than a mile or so along the river bank for food. They did not hunt, made no paths in the forest, and, except to get mates, seemed to need no contact with others and so never sought it. The forest hid them well.

Dafal, a gentle and kind person, took it upon himself to show the People of the Caves new and more varied kinds of food. He taught them to set animal traps, gave them some bows and arrows, a few iron-tipped spears, some simple tools, bits of cloth, and three knives, two of them the long, wide-bladed bolos used everywhere in the Philippines for many purposes.

He taught them to prepare a new food, which he called *natek*. It is made by a complicated process, from the pith of a certain kind of palm tree. With the bolos Dafal had given them, they cut down the palm trees, split them, scooped out the pith, and actually manufactured food. Until that time, they had eaten only what they could pick or catch without traps, hooks, or nets. After they learned to make natek, they came to depend less on the wild yam as their chief food. They find the new food nourishing and tasty. As they themselves say, "We have become fatter."

The Tasaday have abandoned the bows and arrows and the spears for the most part, since they do not seem to want to learn the

Six members of the Tasaday tribe.

skill needed to use them. So far, they have not become good trappers either, and do not set traps often, although they have developed a liking for meat. When they do set traps, they catch wild chickens, monkeys, wild pigs, and once in a while, a deer.

The Tasaday have one serious problem. According to tradition, they may not marry anyone from their own group, and so they must find mates elsewhere. Although they are so isolated, they do have occasional contact with groups even deeper in the forest, and unknown to the outside world. From these groups, they get mates and probably give their own girls as wives. When they are asked where these other people live, they say, "Further in the forest, near a stream," but are not more definite. Nor do they say how long ago they last met with them.

Marriage is a simple affair. The members of the tribe stand around the couple and say, "Beautiful!", then the couple promises to live together and help each other until their hair turns white.

There are no other rituals, and no religious ceremonies. No one outside the tribe has been able to learn whether or not the Tasaday have any religion. They talk only of one unfriendly creature, an ugly bird they have never seen, that lives in another, supernatural world. They do not appear to be afraid of this bird. They are afraid only of snakes, thunder, and lightning.

For several years, Dafal was almost the only person outside their own group who had ever seen a Tasaday. Then, a few people from other tribes also got to know them and learned a little of their language. In 1971, Dafal took a bold step. He had heard from visitors to his village that PANAMIN was searching for hidden tribes. Through these visitors he sent word that he knew of such a tribe, the Tasaday, and would like to tell Elizalde about them. The chief of PANAMIN, excited by this information, thereupon made plans to seek out the Tasaday.

Since Elizalde first met them in 1971, he has become their trusted friend and protector. When they hear the sound of his helicopter, "the big bird," they leave whatever they are doing and head for the clearing where it is to land. He is indeed their bringer of good fortune. He brings medicine to cure a skin disease, ringworm, from which some of them suffer, and has given them some iron tools and demonstrated their use. They have abandoned the easily-broken wooden digging stick and use the bolo to pry the wild yam from the ground. Although the Tasaday still know how to make stone hammers and scrapers, they seldom do so now.

Elizalde has taught them to count, for they did not know how. They never needed to, since one day is like another, and one year like the year before it, in this tropical region. Nor do they have to count their possessions, because all things are shared. Now, although they still have no real need for the skill, they take great delight in counting.

But more important than bringing these changes, PANAMIN has induced the government to declare 55,000 acres of the forest a national reserve. All logging has been stopped in this part of the forest, and very few outsiders are given permission to enter the reserve. Those who do may not bring in tools or presents unless approved by PANAMIN. For this government agency does not wish the Tasaday to be pushed into a way of life for which they are not prepared and may not want.

The Tasaday are bright and alert, and have learned much from the anthropologists who have come to study how Stone Age man lives. When they see ways of making their lives more comfortable, they are quick to adopt them.

Once, their caves were completely bare and the floors dusty and sooty from their fires. Now, for sitting and sleeping, they build low platforms spread with bamboo and split bark, as they had seen the anthropologists do in their tents. After seeing them build racks above the fire for drying out the damp jungle firewood, the Tasaday built similar racks in their caves.

It is too soon to know how much their lives will be affected as a result of having seen what, to them, are great wonders. They have seen helicopters, cameras, transistor radios, short wave radio transmitters and receivers, and generators to power them. And, in 1972, a television broadcasting company from the United States was given permission to film the story of how the Tasaday live. Yet in spite of all of this, there has so far been little change in their main way of life. The men have hinted, however, that perhaps PANAMIN can bring in wives for them so that they do not have to go to distant tribes for mates.

PANAMIN, seeing the Tasaday happy, laughing, singing, making play out of the work of getting food, hopes the tribe stays very much as it is, secure in its own territory. But whether the children will be content, as they grow up, to remain living in caves, no one can tell as yet.

Tasaday children, Lobo and Udo, with a television reporter.

2

A Tribe of Lost Hope
The Ik of Uganda

A WEAK OLD woman has dragged herself into the woods near the village and found a handful of berries. She puts them into her mouth, and before she can swallow them two boys of six who had followed her stealthily attack her. One holds her arms while the other pries open her mouth, puts his fingers in, and scoops out the berries. He and his friend share the meager food.

No one comes to the aid of the old woman. In this tribe, the Ik of Uganda, nobody helps anyone else. Each person thinks only of himself, his ever-present hunger, and ways to satisfy it.

The Ik were not always like this. For many hundreds of years they lived in the northeastern mountains of Uganda. There they roamed freely, hunting animals, and gathering fruits, nuts, and berries for food. They lived in temporary grass huts, traveled in small bands, cooperated in the hunt, and shared the kill. Men and women of one band considered themselves brothers and sisters, and the children, although each knew his own family, were cared for by all the adults. There was love, kindness, and helpfulness among them. All this is now past.

The land of the Ik teemed with wildlife, among them baboons, leopards, hyenas, elephants, and different kinds of antelopes. Ostriches ran across the open spaces, and brightly feathered birds flitted among the trees. Because many of these animals are found only in a few places in the world, in 1939 the Uganda government set the region aside as the Kidepo National Park, in the hope of attracting cash-paying visitors. So that the national park would become profitable, its wildlife had to be protected, and therefore all hunting was forbidden. The Ik thus lost their hunting grounds, and the only means they knew of finding most of their food.

To make sure the Ik did not hunt unlawfully, the government took stern steps. The tribe was forced into a small corner of northeastern Uganda bordering on Kenya and Sudan. There, in exchange for their hunting grounds, they were given land to farm.

But the Ik were not farmers. Besides, the mountainous land is poor, rainfall is scarce, and drought frequent. They were able to scratch only a few meager crops out of the soil. In despair, they turned to begging from the police at the government post, and stealing from each other. They gave up hope of ever having enough to eat.

There are about 2000 IK today. They are blacks. They are short, about five feet tall, and because of constant lack of food most of them are so thin that their bones stand out sharply.

In the Ik territory, days are warm, and although nights are cool, most of the Ik men are naked. Some throw a piece of cloth across one shoulder and use it as a cloak, a towel, a sack, or for any other purpose they choose. A tuft of animal fur or a bright feather worn in the hair completes the men's costume. Sometimes an Ik wears a pair of trousers or a shirt he has received from a missionary or from one of the police officers in the government post nearby.

Except for a small apron, the women too are usually naked. Girls wear an apron of beads, married women one of animal skin. Some, like the men, use a piece of cloth as a cape. Most of the girls and women wear necklaces and earrings of seeds, bits of stone, or pieces of ostrich-egg shells.

Their villages are usually built on hilltops. Each village is surrounded by a stockade made of poles tied closely together with rope made of vines or strips of bark. Only two or three openings, so low that a person must stoop to enter, break through the wall.

Scattered inside the stockade are a number of smaller round stockades. Each of these encloses the compound, or area, in which a

A girl in the unused kitchen area of her family compound. *Colin Turnbull*

family lives. The openings in these family stockades are often so low and narrow that a medium-sized man can barely wriggle through.

There is a reason for making the entrances so small. An Ik is extremely suspicious of anyone who wants to come into his compound. He thinks that anyone who does, comes to steal or do him some other harm. And since a person must just about crawl in, he enters slowly. Thus, those living in the compound have plenty of time to see who is coming. One man told an anthropologist who was visiting the tribe, "This is to give time to put a spear through your neck if we don't like you."

An Ik tries to keep out unwelcome visitors in another way. He builds false entrances leading to a blind alley where a person can be trapped and beaten. There are compounds whose stockades and low-hanging roofs hold spears that are cleverly camouflaged. A stranger who does not know where these spears are hidden would be pierced if he tried to enter the compound.

Each compound houses one family—a man, his wife, and their very young children. The huts, like the stockades, are round, and are made of poles tightly lashed together. An Ik usually smears the walls with mud which, when dried, helps keep out rain and wind.

Cone-shaped thatched roofs top the huts. Toward the back, a sleeping platform helps keep the sleepers dry at times of heavy rain.

Many of the compounds have a small outside cooking area, surrounded by a low wall. The cooking area holds a few stones for a fireplace, some woven baskets, and one or two clay pots for cooking, should there be anything to cook.

Perhaps in the hope that some day there may be food to store, most compounds boast a granary. It looks like a great basket of reeds and poles, standing on stilts. Its cover is hinged to open outward—but it is rarely opened, for there is no need to do so. The granary is almost always empty.

This is the great cry of the Ik: "We are hungry." Birds, caterpillars, and baboons eat most of the sad-looking crops before they are harvested. Discouraged, the Ik neglect the farms, since, they say, their work brings little reward.

When the tomatoes, leafy vegetables, pumpkins, and tobacco they do plant ripen, an Ik picks what he can eat at one time. He steals away and, in secret, gorges himself. Seldom does he bring any back to his family. In the scramble for food among the Ik, each person must find his or her own.

Berries, wild fruit, and even seeds beaten from the heads of grass clumps help still the hunger of an Ik. But again, the person who finds any bolts it down so he can have it all to himself. The fruits and berries have some natural moisture and so are easy to swallow, but the grass seed is dry. Yet, so afraid is an Ik that he may have to share his food, and even though he knows he may get severe stomach cramps as a result, he usually swallows the seed without water.

Termites are a much sought-after food of the Ik. African termites build great mounds in which they nest. Many are taller than a man, and have uneven, weird shapes with many openings. To trap the insects, two or three Ik, usually women working together, spread a closely woven fiber net over the mound. One small opening is left in the net. Over this, they tie a fiber bag, then they beat the mound with sticks. The termites rush from the mound through the opening, their only means of escape, but are trapped in the bag. When cooked, the termites make a nourishing meal.

The Ik are notorious, cunning, and skillful cattle thieves. They themselves raise no cattle, but they steal the animals from neighboring herders. Because of their skill, other more prosperous tribes seek their service to organize cattle raids from neighboring groups. The Ik act as spies and guides, leading raiders to places where little-protected cattle are grazing.

The raiders often turn the stolen animals over to the Ik to hide for them. The Ik drive the cattle to a remote place and keep them there until the raiders think it is safe to reclaim the animals. For this service, the Ik are paid in food, tobacco, shells, and trinkets. As expected, some cows and bulls are missing when the raiders return to collect their loot, but not much is said about this. It is understood that these "lost" animals are part payment for the Ik's services.

There is very little work the Ik do besides arranging raids, a little bit of careless farming, and food-gathering. For the most part, they just sit around idly and hopelessly. In farming, they use a digging-stick and a small hoe with an iron blade, which they get from neighboring tribes. Some of the Ik men make iron spearheads from scrap iron for themselves and for other groups, but strangely, they use stone hammers and other stone tools to do this. In fact, except for the iron spearheads and hoe blades, practically all of their tools are of stone.

group of Ik tribesmen
ioning iron spearheads
stone tools. *Colin
nbull*

Their way of kindling a fire has not changed in hundreds, perhaps thousands, of years. They use a fire drill made of two sticks. One, held down on the ground firmly with a foot, has a notch in it. Another stick, resting in the notch, is twirled rapidly with both hands. The friction of the two sticks produces heat, and in only a few minutes a wisp of smoke rises above the notch. Quickly, the firemaker puts some dry grass or leaves at the notch. He blows on the smoking stick, the tinder catches fire and bursts into flame.

Although the Ik tools and method of firemaking have not changed in centuries, their social life has changed completely since they lost their hunting grounds. When they were hunters and gatherers, they came together to celebrate important events in the life of the family. A week after a child was born the father's parents came for a visit. They were feasted, and then gave the child a name. Marriage, too, was the occasion for the gathering together of many bands, feasting and dancing. Now, when a child is born, no one is invited to celebrate. Its parents simply give it a name. Nor is there any marriage feast. A man and woman decide to live together, and set up their home usually in the stockade where the man's family lives.

In the old days, when a person died the body was buried facing east, in a pleasant place with a good view of the mountains. Sometimes the possessions that he particularly liked were buried with him. A whole day of mourning and fasting followed the burial, then a day of somber feasting.

Now, nobody mourns for the dead. Any adult member of the family who is around buries the body secretly in a shallow grave and covers the spot with rocks or dirt. Sometimes no one in the village knows that a person has died until the son is seen wearing beads known to have belonged to his father. To announce openly that someone has died means that the family must provide a funeral feast for the village.

Loving another person—a wife, a husband, or a child, means sharing food and giving help. But since each Ik looks only for his own good, he leaves little room in his life for love or affection. Husband and wife go off, separately, in the morning, to search for food. The woman carries the baby in a fiber cradle tied around her shoul-

Hunger comes to animals and humans alike. Here an Ik boy competes with a young kid for its mother's milk. *Colin Turnbull*

ders, the toddlers trail after her. When they return home in the late afternoon or evening, each goes about his or her own business. Rarely is a meal cooked for the family, for seldom is any brought back.

The Ik children fare badly. They are unloved, just another mouth to feed. So, when they are three or at most, four years old, they are pushed out of the family hut to fend for themselves. Almost never do they enter the hut again, except possibly when grown up. The little boy or girl sometimes stays within the family compound, but outside the hut. If it rains, and there is no other shelter, the child may ask permission to sit in his parents' doorway, but he may not lie down or sleep there.

The wall of each family compound has a small opening only big enough for a child to crawl through. He uses this opening to go to some other compound if he wishes to do so, or to a more central part of the village. There the children band together in two groups, the three- to seven-year-olds in one band, and the eight- to thirteen-year-olds in another. Six to twelve children make up a band. The members of the band usually build a small shelter for themselves within the village stockade.

The child picks for himself another of his own age as a friend. These two children defend each other against the other band members and cooperate in getting food. But these friendships do not last long. When one of the two thinks he can do better by joining up with someone else, he does not hesitate to leave his partner.

For food, the children eat anything they can find or scrounge. Figs, the bark of certain trees, berries and wild fruits make up the bulk of their food. When they are very hungry and can get nothing else, they eat small handfuls of earth, and even swallow small smooth pebbles.

The youngest children in the junior bands, the three and four-year-olds, are of course not much use to the group in fights, in building a shelter, and in other group activities. But if the little ones survive the hunger, disease, and exposure, the older ones know they will become useful in time. Thus they tolerate them, but bully them nevertheless.

When a child in the younger band reaches the age of eight, the others drive him out, and he is forced to join the senior group. He becomes its youngest member, the butt of the jokes of the others, and the victim of their cruel pranks. As he grows older, and a younger child enters the group, its members turn their abuse on this newcomer. The youngest child in each band knows that he must suffer this abuse if he is to remain in the band, since alone he will not stay alive for long.

Even though the parents refuse to give the children food or shelter, they expect those in the senior band to be of some help in what little farming is done. They send the boys and girls out to the fields to drive away animals, birds, and insects that attack the crops. The band feels this gives its members the right to steal ripening plants, but they beat severely any child in a junior band caught stealing from a field. The adults know of this thievery, but they pretend not to. They find there is less loss this way than if they allowed the animal pests to destroy the fields altogether.

Like children everywhere, the young Ik find time to play, but even their games reflect their harsh existence. They play at hunting with toy spears and slingshots, often chasing after younger or weaker children and hurting them. They build small, crude huts

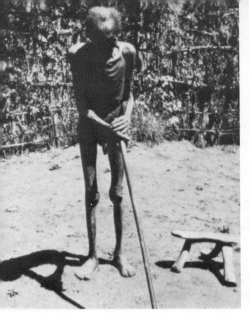
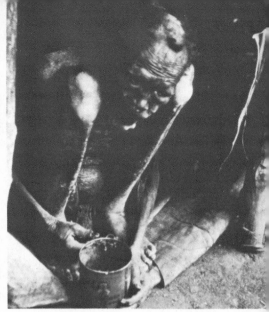

Two old skeleton-thin tribesmen. One jealously guards the bit of food given him by an anthropologist. *Colin Turnbull*

quickly and carelessly, and take pleasure in knocking down each others'. They stick bits of bark and small pebbles into elaborate mud pies as make-believe meat. Since food, even play food, is valuable, a child often eats his mudpie.

So, early in childhood, an Ik learns the selfish and cruel behavior that stays with him for the rest of his life. When he leaves his senior band he makes no other friends. By this time, he has also learned to laugh, not in fun, but at someone else's misfortune.

Anyone who is hurt, sick, or dying gives an Ik cause for amusement. A tiny child crawls toward a fire and knowing no better, puts his hand into the flame. People stand by and burst into laughter at the child's scream of pain, but the mother does not help the child. She pulls it away only after she hears the others laugh. She seems to be glad to have been able to give the onlookers something to laugh about, that may make them forget their own hunger.

The old and weak are great sources of laughter. A blind man tries to reach a dead hyena to get some food for himself. He is knocked down and trampled by men, women and children rushing to get at the carcass before he does. When they see this, they laugh, and the blind man does too.

31

Old people are much worse off than the children. The children live in bands, help each other somewhat and are young enough to scramble around for food. The old are usually too weak even to try to get any. The husband, wife, or grown son or daughter chases the feeble old person out of the hut or compound. He is given no food or water, and left to die.

The Ik have given up all religious rituals of their former life. There are no priests left to perform these rituals, even if the people wanted to. They once believed in a god who lived in the sky and created them. They believed that the souls of their ancestors lived in the sky, too, and like stars watched over them. The Ik, through their priests, turned to their ancestors' souls for help, or to appease them if they offended them. There is one mountain that they called "the place of god," and considered sacred. Most Ik still think so, but the young people do not know why. Only a few old men remember some of the rituals once practiced on the mountain. The Ik now say that since their god has retreated and left them to this miserable life, they have abandoned him.

All of the tribe's past customs, however, have not been lost. Some villages have a medicine man, who uses herbs to try to cure certain illnesses such as colds. To cure a cold, the medicine man uses white clay. He warms the clay, touches it to the patient's forehead, shoulders, and chest. Usually, the cold goes away in about a week—as it might anyway, without this treatment.

At the police station near the Ik villages, the people of the tribe can get some simple medicines, but they seldom bother to come for them. They either remain sick, use a medicine man, recover naturally, or just die.

The Ik have given up all hope for a better future for themselves or their children. Year after year, as hunger kills off more and more people, the tribe becomes smaller. Some few gather up enough strength to move out of their villages, to join other tribes in Kenya or Sudan. In any case, it is likely that before long the tribe will die out as a group.

3

Nomads of the Kalahari Desert
The African Bushmen

IN THE DARK night of the Kalahari Desert in southern Africa, a young mother cradles her infant son in her arms and holds him up to the starry sky. Softly, she begs the stars to replace his childish heart with the heart of a hunter. She knows that when he grows up he will need to be brave and fearless, for here, where the African Bushmen live, the men must be skillful in the hunt. True, most of their food comes from desert plants. But animals supply meat that builds strong bodies and provides hides, sinews, and other necessities the plants cannot furnish.

The Kalahari Desert is a harsh, dry land that stretches from Southwest Africa to western Botswana, an area of about 10,000 square miles. It is not altogether barren, for it is dotted with clumps of tall grass that break through the surface. Some trees and low bushes stand out against the tan of the dry, dusty ground and the blue of the sky. But there are no lakes or streams in the desert. What water there is lies in shallow holes or in little pockets underground, caught there when rain comes in the months of December, January, and February—summer in the Southern Hemisphere. Most of the rain disappears into the thirsty ground almost as soon as it falls.

In these summer months, temperatures may rise as high as 120 degrees by noon. Winter days in June, July, and August are cooler, about 80 degrees at mid-day. But winter nights are sometimes so cold that, if by chance there is some water left standing in the open, it freezes overnight.

The Bushmen once lived in other parts of Africa, in the high plateaus of the east and northeast, in Rhodesia and South Africa. There is ample evidence to show this. Scattered in these parts of the continent, on rock shelters and in shallow caves, there are paintings and engravings of animals, hunters, and dancers. They are like the ones the Bushmen were making as late as 1917. No other people in Africa have been known to do such art work. Thus, scientists are quite sure that the Bushmen lived wherever these pictures are found.

The Bushmen have been living in the Kalahari Desert for about 500 years. They fled into this inhospitable wasteland when first Bantus—a certain group of African blacks—and later, Europeans, overran their land. They killed Bushmen in great numbers and took over their territory for cattle-raising. The Bushmen, gentle, unwarlike people, retreated into the arid Kalahari rather than fight back. They managed to adapt themselves to the life of the desert nomad, hunting and gathering their food in this dry land. At most, about 40,000 Bushmen live there now.

They are short people, averaging five feet in height. Their skin color is yellow-brown, their faces rather flat, with small noses. Short black hair, coiled like tight springs, grows in tufts close to their scalps.

In summer, they have little need for clothing. Most children are naked, and the men usually wear only loin cloths of animal skins. They sometimes also wear a cloak called a *kaross*, made of a single antelope hide. It is tied around the waist with a cord of animal sinews, and knotted at the shoulders so that it forms a carrying pouch. The women wear short skin aprons front and back, and almost always have a kaross. A woman needs one much more than a man does, for in it she carries her baby, food she gathers, a supply of water, and whatever few tools she may need as she wanders in the desert. In the winter, everybody who can get one, wears a cloak made of hide as protection against the evening cold.

Although their clothing is sparse, Bushmen women, and some men, wear necklaces of small pieces of ostrich eggshells strung on animal sinews. They also make necklaces from thin sections of

34

Bushmen outside their shelter. *American Museum of Natural History*

dried reeds and brown seed pods. Many women deck themselves out with headbands of pieces of ostrich eggshells, fringed with eggshell beads. Both men and women wear leather or bark arm and leg bands, on the upper arm and just below the knee.

Water is too precious to use for washing, so Bushmen seldom do, except in the rainy season. They rub fat into their bodies to keep their skin from drying out, and dust themselves with a sweet-smelling powder made from certain leaves and wood. Because they rarely wash themselves with the scant water, their skin looks darker than it actually is. When they perspire heavily, lighter patches of true skin color show.

Bushmen speak a language that is very difficult for an outsider to understand, and even harder to learn to pronounce. The words have many combinations of sharp plops and clicks made with the tongue and quick short sucking sounds. In all the world, only three other groups of people, and these too are in Africa, speak in this way.

Because food for a large group is impossible to find at any one time in the desert, Bushmen live in small bands of 15 to 40 persons. A band is made up of a headman or chief, his wife or wives and children, perhaps his brothers and their families, and his wives' families. The other men often have more than one wife, too. There is no hard and fast rule about who may join a band, except that all members must be closely related to someone in it.

The band camps in one place for a few days, and when the food they can gather within easy distance is exhausted, it moves on. The headman, who inherits his position from his father, leads the band from one encampment to another. He has no power over the band, and receives no special privilege or extra food.

Although Bushmen have no permanent homes, a band has what it calls its "own place," near a water hole. Here it spends most of the rainless winter months, leaving it only for a day or two at a time to gather food. The "little rains," mostly thunderstorms, come in September, and the band moves away in search of fresh plant foods that have now begun to grow.

A band moves in an area of about 70 miles which it considers its own territory. The Bushmen know just where patches of certain

Bushmen women fill ostrich eggshells with water for future use. *American Museum of Natural History*

plants ripen each time of the year, and head for that spot at the proper time.

In their kaross, the women carry ostrich eggshells they have filled with water through a hole in one end. The hole is plugged with grass to keep the water from spilling or evaporating. But since this may not supply a band with enough water in its wanderings, the people prepare for such an emergency ahead of time. When they have some to spare, they bury water-filled ostrich eggshells in caches along the route they take each year. They know where this water supply is stored, and that it will be there when they need it. No Bushman ever takes a water-filled shell that he himself has not hidden. He knows that a band is counting on this water cache, and the life of its people may depend on it. Just as he would not want to find his own cache stolen, so he would never steal another's.

To avoid using up the stored water unless absolutely necessary, a Bushman, when roaming the desert, looks for a patch of grass that often sprouts above underground water. If his keen eyes spot one, out comes the hollow drinking reed he always carries with him. He puts a grass filter into one end, pushes that end down into the ground, and begins to suck. He may have to suck until his lips are sore before he gets a drink, but he almost always succeeds. He may even get out enough water to fill an empty ostrich eggshell.

When a band reaches its day's destination, the women start building the encampment. Each woman makes a shelter for her own family. First, she looks for a shallow depression, or scoops one out, near some grass and if possible in the shade of a bush or tree. She lines the hollow with grass, on which her family will sleep. Sometimes this is its only shelter, and because the people lie slightly below the surface, they are protected from the wind. A few sticks stuck in the ground around the family "home" marks it off from the others, and a bent pole is its doorway.

More often, the women push branches or twigs into the ground around the hollow, and use them as a four or five-foot-high framework which they cover with grass. Until the wind blows the grass away, the family has a cover over its head. Inside, if it is cold, there is a small fire for warmth.

Separate huts are built for the children who are strong enough to go about by themselves. All the boys sleep together in one hut, or in some bands, under a tree that is in the center of the encampment. The girls live in another hut, with an old woman who is entrusted with their care.

It does not take long to build the shelters. As soon as they are finished, the women go out to gather food. They take along sharp-pointed digging sticks three or four feet long, and walk slowly, scrutinizing the ground. They see an almost invisible dry thread of a vine, which they follow until it disappears into the soil. Here they begin digging, and pull up a fat, juicy root. One kind, called a *bi,* looks like a big, hairy gray beet with a hard crust that keeps the fleshy part from drying out. When they get back to the camp, the roots they have found will be scraped with a wooden knife, the scrapings squeezed to get out the juice, and the solid material eaten too.

The women know that under a certain tiny crack in the ground, a kind of mushroom grows. They dig it up and put it into their kaross. Into this pouch go a few bean-like seeds, nuts, berries, and small, spiny cucumbers less than three inches long, tasty and full of moisture.

38

The girls go along with the old woman of their hut, and she teaches them the skills they need to have to provide food for their families when they grow up. They look upon her as a wise grandmother, a teacher, and a friend, one they love and respect.

The season when the tsama melons are ripe is the time of the year when there is almost no water to be had anywhere in the desert. Luckily, the pulpy fruit of the melon supplies both the Bushmen and the animals with liquid. The tasma melon is about the size and shape of a cantalope, with a shiny pale green rind. A Bushman gets the most out of the melon by cutting a hole in the top, inserting a stick, mashing up the pulp until it is quite liquid, and taking a drink. He eats what is left of the pulp. Every part is used. The seeds are roasted and eaten, or ground into a kind of flour. The rind, when dried out, makes pots, bowls, and containers for loose objects.

While the women are out gathering plants the men hunt animals. Each man takes his young sons along to teach them to hunt. At first the boys are given small wooden bows and arrows, and when they have mastered these, are given full-sized weapons. By the time a boy is 14 or 15 years old he has usually learned to hunt like an adult.

In hunting, the men sometimes make simple snares to catch small game, but usually this particular means is left to the boys. The men use a throwing stick—a club of hard wood about three feet long, with a rounded knob at one end, to knock down birds and small animals. For some game, they use spears. But to kill larger animals such as hartebeests, wildebeasts, antelopes, and giraffes, they use bows and arrows. The arrows are small and unfeathered, and so not very accurate, but accuracy does not matter much because they are tipped with a powerful poison.

Some poison is made from snake venom and some from plants, beetles, and spiders. But the most commonly used poison comes from the pupa of a certain insect. In this resting stage the insect is simply squeezed onto the arrow point. If the men find more of these insects than they can use at the time, they dry them out and later, when needed, grind them into a powder in the hollow part of a neckbone of a giraffe. They mix the powder with the juice of a special plant and roll the arrow point in the gummy mass. The men use great care not to get any of the poison into their eyes or on a cut in their skin, because once it gets into their blood stream, it is fatal.

In some bands, before going out to hunt, the men disguise themselves in ostrich feathers or animal skins. They think this will act as a camouflage when they stalk the game. Bushmen hunt any animal that roams the desert, except hyenas and baboons. They will not eat hyenas because these animals eat dead bodies of people, and baboons because they call them "people who sit on their heels."

The hunters approach animals in a silent, crouching run, and when no more than fifty feet away shoot off their poisoned arrows. It may take several hours, sometimes a day or two after it has been shot, before the poison takes full effect and the animal dies.

The men trail it and when they find its carcass, skin it on the spot. They cut it open and clean it, collect the blood in bags made from the stomach, then slice up the rest and bring it back to the camp. There is no danger that the arrow poison will harm a person who eats any part of the animal, because the poison, to do its damage, must enter the blood stream through a cut in a blood vessel.

The meat is divided among all the members of the band, and each person gets a fair share. No part of the animal is wasted. If it is suitable, the skin is used for a kaross. Otherwise, it is made into quivers, loin cloths, aprons, sandals, and pouches for such things as seeds and powder. Sinews make bowstrings, cord and string from which netted bags are knotted. Bones are made into arrow shafts, knives, and awls. Even the horns are put to use as spoons, scoops, and whistles. If there is any meat left, it is smoked to preserve it for a time when there will be none.

Each family has its own fire for cooking, which only the men are allowed to make. They use friction sticks to get sparks and dried grass as tinder. The women stay by their own fires. If they want to talk to each other, they shout across the camp, because the husbands say their wives must stay at home, and not gad about.

Some time during the evening, one of the men may take out a small drum or a five-stringed instrument called a *guashi*. Then the rhythm and the music break the stillness of the desert night. The songs seldom have words, but they have names that express the hardships, and also the joys, of the life of desert nomad.

A Bushman sights his quarry and takes aim. *Wide World Photos*

After a few days in a camp, the band gets ready to move on. Their belongings are few. The man takes his spear, bow and arrows, fire sticks, water reed, some odds and ends which he puts into a string bag. The woman tucks her digging stick and water reed into her belt and puts small objects into tortoise-shell or melon-rind containers. These go into her kaross, together with her mortar and pestle, her wooden pot, and her baby. They go on to a new location, where, once more, they build shelters, soon exhaust the food supply, and wander on.

When a person dies, the other family members tie the body into a sitting position and wrap it in an old kaross. They put it into a grave that they have dug with their digging sticks, and fill the grave with thorny branches to protect the body from hyenas, who would devour it.

There may come a time when food and water are extremely scarce, and the whole band is threatened with death from starvation. Then, anyone who holds back the band in its trek to search for food endangers the lives of all. The very old and weak, who cannot be carried, are the ones who would fall behind. If such a situation arises, Bushmen very reluctantly take a drastic step to preserve the lives of the majority of the band. They build a shelter for the old, give them what food and water can possibly be spared, and, with much weeping, leave them. They will do this only when otherwise there is no hope for survival for the rest. The aged know they will die of heat, hunger, thirst, or attack by animals, but they accept this as a way of life—and death—in the desert.

Almost a year after it has left, a band gets back to its own place. Here they have closer contact with other bands than while roaming the desert. This is when Bushmen exchange information about the location of certain plants, waterholes, or herds of animals. It is the time when a person can most easily leave one band if he so wishes, and join another in which he has a close relative. And, since marriage between members of the same band is forbidden, it is the time to find a wife or a husband.

A suitor, to gain the consent of a girl's father, must show he can take care of her. He does this by bringing a present of an animal he has killed. But a girl is not forced into a marriage she does not want. Bushmen make a kind of game of finding out whether or not a girl finds a suitor welcome. He comes to her camp and tries to take her away by force, while she is supposed to resist him. The men in her band help her by showering blows upon him. If she does not pull back very hard, and lets the young man hold her arm, it means she consents to the marriage. But if she frees herself from him, it is her way of telling him to look elsewhere for a wife.

A feast follows if the girl shows she is willing to marry the man. If she is his first wife, the couple lives with her band until they

42

have three children or are old enough to have had them. Then they live with the band of their choice, usually the husband's. A second wife goes to live with her husband's band.

The Bushmen's religion is a very simple one. They believe there is a Great First Spirit who looks after them. When the land is particularly dry, they perform dances to draw his attention to the lack of rain. They believe the stars to be hunters, as Bushmen are, and pray to them and to the moon, too, to help in the hunt.

When a person becomes very sick, Bushmen arrange a medicine dance in the hope that this will drive out the illness. Very often, several bands get together to perform it. The dance is a social event,

Bushmen sing and dance around their campfire. *Wide World Photos*

as well as a curing ritual. It goes on all night, with the people talking, joking, eating, and sometimes going off for a nap between dances.

The women and girls sit in a circle, sing and clap their hands. The men and boys dance outside the circle in rhythm to the songs. The men shake rattles made of gourds, and wear anklets of seed pods, dry cocoons, or strings of pieces of ostrich eggshells, which clatter as they dance.

The life that the Bushmen have made for themselves has kept the group alive these hundreds of years, but it is changing. When Europeans and Bantus established farms and cattle ranges closer to the desert, they induced many of the Bushmen to come to work for them. There, in the homes and fields, the desert nomads saw products they had never seen before. They discovered enamelled and aluminum pots, iron and glass they could make into arrows and spear points, and the use of tobacco. They learned that the farmers were willing to give them glass beads and wire in exchange for skins of desert animals, ostrich feathers and eggshell necklaces. Now, many Bushmen smoke tobacco, use iron or glass points for their arrows and spears, and wear glass bead necklaces as well as those made from eggshells. Their arm and leg bands are often made of many strands of wire instead of sinew or animal hide.

There are many Bushmen who find the less rigorous life outside the desert very attractive. They marry Bantus, adopt their life style, and never return to the Kalahari Desert.

However, a great many others cling to the pattern of life their fathers knew. They work for a while, then come back to the desert, their own way of life and their own people. There have been changes in their lives, and undoubtedly there will be more, as wells are dug and more land is taken over for cattle grazing. The bands will probably become fewer as more Bushmen leave the desert, but there are always likely to be some who prefer the freedom and openness of the desert to the more enclosed life of the outside world.

4

Head-Hunters of the Amazon
The Jívaro

A RADIO IN THE village of Shuar in eastern Ecuador blares out a song in the language of the Jivaro Indians. It is followed by a song in Spanish.

A young man brings to his village a foot-pedal sewing machine he has bought with money he earned working as a roadbuilder. His father watches in amazement as his son sews a seam. The father tries to operate the machine, and after a few attempts, succeeds. He stares at the fine, even, tight stitches in wonder at how easy work can become.

Missionaries and government agents are bringing a totally new way of life to many of the Jivaro (HEE-var-oh) Indians, the dreaded headhunters of the Amazon jungle. The Indians who live near the edges of the jungle, and who have met many white men, usually welcome these changes. However, deep in the forest, remote from white men, there are still fierce Jivaro head-hunters who raid villages, kill the men, and shrink their severed heads.

Spanish explorers looking for gold first came upon these Indians in the middle of the 16th century. At first some of the Indians cooperated with the explorers in their search for gold. But the ever-increasing greediness and cruelty of the Spaniards led the Indians to a bloody revolt in 1599. They massacred the white men and the few who escaped brought back tales of horror and savagery on the part of the Indians they called Jivaros, meaning "the savage ones." Although these Indians call themselves the Shuar, they are still usually known as the Jivaro.

Fearful for their lives, the white men left the Jivaros alone after that time, in the jungle on the eastern slope of the Andes Mountains. Only one small settlement of gold miners was established, at the edge of the jungle, and gave the Indians their only contact with white men. The Jivaros remained hostile toward these settlers until about the middle of the 1800's. By then, realizing they could profit by trade, they began to exchange salt, pigs, and later, shrunken heads as souvenirs, for the steel machetes and the cloth of the white men.

Gradually, other white settlers, mostly cattle-raisers and missionaries, moved into the fringe areas of the forest. By the middle of the 1900's a good deal of trade was being carried on between whites and the Jivaros. Shotguns became prized items received in exchange for forest products. But most of the Jivaros living in the deep interior of the jungle have no contact with white men. However, almost all of them now have some of the white man's goods—steel knives, cloth, machetes, and rifles. They get them through a chain of trading that starts with a Jivaro living in a fringe village. He buys the goods and exchanges them with a trading partner who usually lives in a different neighborhood. The partner in turn carries these goods to another village, and this kind of exchange goes on until a whole network of trade is established. The people who are the last to own the goods may have no idea of where these things came from in the first place.

The land of the Jivaros is mountainous and heavily forested. Streams, rapids, and waterfalls abound. Here are the headwaters of the mighty Amazon River. The steep slope of the Andes to the west and the rushing waters act as effective barriers against invaders. Within this vast area live about 11,000 Jivaros, 8,000 at the fringes, and the rest in the interior.

Where the Jivaros came from is unknown. Since their language is somewhat like that of certain other South American Indians, they probably, at one time, lived among them. Scientists think they have been living in the jungle for about 2,500 years.

A Jivaro tribesman wearing face paint and headdress. *Museum of the American Indian, Heye Foundation*

The Jivaros have the appearance of other American Indians—copper-colored skin, high cheekbones, straight black hair, and a fold in the upper eyelids that make the eyes look slanty. They are short and stocky, about five feet four inches tall. They cut their hair in straight bangs across their foreheads, and allow it to grow long at the sides and back.

Both men and women, especially in the interior, wear very little clothing. The men wrap a simple coarse homespun cotton skirt around the lower part of their body and tie it at the waist with a string or belt. Two lengths of similar cloth make up a woman's dress. The pieces are sewn together only at the right shoulder, hang down in front and back, and are circled at the waist with a belt.

This is the everyday costume of the men and women. But when receiving visitors, the men usually put on skirts of machine-made cloth, and "trade" shirts. A few have trousers for dress wear. For company, the women change into dresses of finer cotton machine cloth, but the style remains the same, tied at the right shoulder and held together at the waist.

47

In the use of feathers and paint, the Jivaro men show their love of ornamentation. Most men wear tasselled headbands into which are woven brilliant toucan feathers, and paint both their faces and bodies with bright red pigment made from ground-up achiote seeds. So concerned are the men with their appearance, that they almost always carry a cosmetic pouch containing brushes and paint for a quick touch-up. The women, on the other hand, rarely if ever use body paint.

Five, perhaps ten families, living in houses as much as a mile from each other, make up a Jivaro community. Such small groups cannot really be called villages, but rather, neighborhoods. There is no head man of the community, nor any other kind of official.

A Jivaro builds his house beside a small stream, on a low hill. Neighbors often help him in its construction. First, he makes a clearing in the forest, large enough so that his wives—for he usually has two or three—can plant a vegetable garden.

The house is oval-shaped, about 25 feet wide and twice as long. Its walls are seven feet high, made of poles set into the ground about an inch apart, and lashed together with strips of bark. A thatched roof rises to a high peak. Heavy wooden doors, one at each end, are held securely in place by means of crossbars.

The Jivaros need a house as big as this, because all their councils, visiting, celebrations, and dancing takes place inside. Were they to hold them outside, they would be vulnerable to attack from other groups.

About nine persons live in each house. It is divided into men's quarters at one end, and women and children's quarters at the other. A widowed mother also has a place there. The house is kept neat and clean. It has beds made of palm slats, with small fireplaces at the foot of each. High platforms for pottery and other breakables keep these safely out of the reach of small children. There are also a few stools for themselves and visitors. Each house has several small chicken coops spaced along the walls, in which the birds are kept both for their meat and their eggs.

A house is occupied for eight or nine years, until it rots, or game near it becomes scarce, or nearby wood for fires is used up. Then the family moves a few miles away and builds a new one.

Planting the garden, cultivating it, and harvesting the crop is done by the women, with the help of the children. They grow corn, sweet potatoes, squash, peanuts, bananas, tobacco, and cotton. The most abundant crop is a big root vegetable called manioc, from which they make soups, small round cakes and beer. Tremendous quantities of beer are consumed, as much as three or four gallons a day for the men, one or two a day for the women, and about half a gallon for children nine or ten years old. It is not very strong beer, since it is allowed to ferment for only four or five days, but consumed in such quantities, it has a potent effect.

The women use only a few tools in gardening—a pointed planting stick for making holes in the ground for seed, a flat-bladed stick for digging root vegetables, and a steel machete to harvest plants and to cut weeds. In spite of their work, after about three years, the garden becomes overgrown with weeds in this jungle climate. It is abandoned, and the men clear a new piece of ground nearby.

Only the women make pottery and prepare food. Spinning, weaving, and basket-making are done by men, never by women, for a particular reason. The Jivaros believe that all objects, living and non-living, have a soul that is either male or female. Women cook because fruits, fire, and the clay of pots have female souls. Men do their kind of work because cotton, looms, and basket fiber have male souls. However, since the machete is not originally a Jivaro object, but is obtained in trade with white men, it has no soul and may be used by both men and women.

The machete serves many purposes. It is used to cut a new clearing, to dig root crops such as manioc, for woodworking, digging clay for pottery, preparing food, felling trees, and cutting hair.

This is about the only metal tool most Jivaros have. They make needles from monkey-leg bones; mortarboards and pestles for grinding manioc are of wood; the pots, dippers, and cups are of clay or hollowed-out gourds. Jars holding ten to 13 gallons, for fermenting beer, are also made of clay.

More important than their work around the hut, the men supply the family with meat and fish. They hunt monkeys and birds, wild hogs, ocelots, armadillos, and other forest animals. In hunting, they

49

A hunter with his blowgun. The quiver around his neck holds poison darts.
Museum of the American Indian, Heye Foundation

use two kinds of weapons, a shotgun that they get by trading animal skins, and a blowgun. They do not make the blowguns themselves, but get them from a neighboring tribe, the Achuara, who are experts in this craft.

The blowgun is a hollow wooden tube about seven feet long. Through this tube, the hunter shoots out a small, thin dart made from the rib of a palm leaf. Its sharp point is tipped with curare, a deadly poison.

The hunter carries the darts in a quiver around his neck, or sticks them through his hair just above his ears where he can get them easily. The blowgun can send a dart swiftly and silently for 40 to 50 feet, and a good hunter can blow a dart as far as 100 feet.

At least one dog accompanies the hunter on most occasions. Sometimes, a man takes a wife with him on an expedition, to manage the dogs on their leashes. She is usually the youngest wife.

A man values his dogs so much that very often one of his wives nurses a puppy along with her own child. The dog is carefully trained and when it is considered ready for its first hunt, its owner holds a three-day ceremony which admits the dog to "adulthood."

Every household has two or three dogs. They serve their

owners in other ways besides hunting. In the gardens, they kill rodents which would otherwise gnaw away and destroy the crops. At night, they are chained to the foot of the wives' beds to bark at the approach of an enemy.

As for the children, they are allowed little time for play. When a girl is about four years old, she is taught to take care of the baby, to keep the hut clean, to work in the garden, and to make pottery. The boys are taught to use the blowgun, to hunt, and to help their fathers in other ways.

A Jivaro parent puts his child to work early, for he thinks that unless he does so, the child will turn into a lazy adult. Boys and girls are also discouraged from joking and laughing even though the adults may, because the parents believe this leads the children to become liars when they are grown.

There is, however, one kind of recreation in which the children are encouraged. They are taught to splash and bathe in the running streams and to swim. Swimming, for people living in this jungle, is much more than play, however. Knowing how to do so is a necessity, since, in traveling about, there are many streams too deep to be crossed on foot.

A girl marries when she is very young. Because the women do so much work for the family, they are in great demand as wives. To make sure he will have at least one young, strong wife, a man sometimes "reserves" a girl for himself when she is still a child. He does this by giving her parents presents of featherwork or trade goods. If he wishes, he may then take her to his own house to be raised by his other wives until she is ready for marriage. If she is very unhappy there, she may return to her parents' home.

A girl is never forced into a marriage. When a man wants a certain girl for a wife, if he has not already reserved her, he sends a kinsman to her father to ask for her. The father consults with the girl and her mother, and if they consent the man comes to stay overnight in the men's quarters of her house. Early in the morning he goes out to hunt birds and monkeys to impress her family with his ability to provide for her, and offers her the game to cook. If by now she is certain she wants to become his wife, she sits down beside him and joins him in eating the cooked food. They are now considered married.

The couple live in the house of the girl's family until their first child is born. The girl helps her mother, and the husband works with his father-in-law in hunting, gathering firewood, and in his other tasks. However, if the man has another wife and his own house, he takes his new wife back with him, but pays her father a bride price of a shotgun or other trade goods to make up for the loss of his services.

Because the Jivaros do not live close together, children have very little contact with those from other families. They learn from their fathers that almost everybody is hostile and treacherous, and that they must constantly be on the alert for enemy attack.

For the Jivaros are a people full of suspicion and hate. Most mornings, the father gathers his sons around him and recites to them his personal hatreds. He names those who he thinks have wronged or insulted him or have killed members of his family. He does this to keep alive in his sons the hate he feels, and his desire for revenge.

When a man's hatred toward another Jivaro finally builds up to high pitch, he plans a raid to assassinate that person. First, he goes

Jivaro women busy preparing food. *Museum of the American Indian, Heye Foundation*

to a man called a *kakaram,* or "powerful one." This is a man known for his skill in organizing raids and for the many people he has killed. The kakaram sends out scouts to recruit others to join in the venture. There are always men willing to go along, either because they want to be in his good graces, or because they too hate the intended victim, or because they want to secure for themselves a man's head.

Killing a man and cutting off his head, then shrinking it, is a most important affair in the life of the jungle Jivaros. For they believe that a boy, when he is in his early teens, acquires a soul that stays with him for only four or five years. Then it leaves his body, and he must get a new one. When he kills a man, the victim's soul enters his body and again, remains for several years. Thus a Jivaro, every few years, must go on an expedition to capture a new soul for himself. There is at least one killing raid a year. Many raids are not for revenge, but for the sole purpose of obtaining heads, and thus, souls. Girls and women are not thought to have souls, and so are not involved in head-hunting.

Once a raid has been decided upon, the participants build a large house in which they will hold a feast afterwards. The raid itself takes place just before dawn. The men steal through the forest to the huts of the enemy, and when close, start firing shotguns. The victims are usually caught by surprise, for the secret of where the raid is to take place has been well kept.

A dead man's head is cut off, tied around the killer's neck, and dangles down his back. When the raiders reach a safe distance from the victim's hut, they start the process of making a *tsantsa,* a shrunken head.

First, they cut a slit up the rear of the scalp, remove the whole skin, and discard the skull. Next they boil the skin for half an hour, and it shrinks to about half its size. It is then dried, cleaned, the slit sewn up, and the lips tied together.

Five or six heated stones are now put into the sack formed by the skin, and rolled around in it to make the head shrink still further. When the stones cool, they are removed and the process is repeated. Finally, the neck opening becomes too small for the stones, and hot sand is poured through the opening instead.

53

The raiding party moves on toward its home ground. Each day, for several hours, the hot sand process is repeated, and the skin is rubbed with charcoal to blacken it. By the time the raiders have returned home, about six days later, the skin has shrunk to about the size of a big orange. A hole is made in the top, and a double string passed through it. The hardened, blackened tsantsa, black hair flowing down, lips tied, can now hang around the neck of its captor. He wears it as a decoration for years, or hangs it in his house as a keepsake.

Tsantsas are in great demand by white men, as curios, but the government of Ecuador has forbidden their sale. However, some do reach the market by illegal means. In the cities, souvenir shops sell what the owners claim are real tsantsas, but they are almost always fakes, made from leather.

Three great feasts follow a tsantsa raid, the first in the hut prepared for it. The men who have captured a head give two more. Men and women dance to the music of flutes and drums made from monkey skins. Tremendous amounts of food and beer are consumed, and hallucinogenic jungle plants taken to induce strange visions. Sometimes a man must give the third feast more than a year after the raid, because he has to build himself a bigger house for his many guests, and clear a bigger garden for the food and beer his wives will serve.

Because a Jivaro fears that at some time he, too, will be the victim of a head-hunting raid, he takes precautions to protect his home. At night, the doors to his hut are heavily barred, and the dogs inside the house trained to bark out warning of a trespasser.

For further security, he often conceals traps near his hut. One type is a pit about four feet deep and three feet square. Sharp lances tipped with poison stick up from the bottom. A stranger, unaware of the trap, may fall into it and be killed or severely wounded. Another type is made of a number of spikes hidden in the trees, and aimed at the face and chest of an intruder. A liana vine across the trail acts as a trigger, and releases the spikes when someone steps on it. Now that most Jivaros have firearms, they sometimes hide a loaded shotgun in the bushes and attach a string to its trigger. They stretch the string across the path to their homes and when someone steps on

A large, fist-sized Tsanta, or shrunken head. *Museum of the American Indian, Heye Foundation*

it, the gun goes off. The members of the family know where all the traps are placed and make sure to avoid them.

The belief that a man gets a new soul from someone he has killed is the most important religious belief of the Jivaros, but it is not the only one. They believe that there is an Earth Mother who is responsible for the growth of crops. She stays in the garden, and dances in it during the night as long as it is well weeded. Therefore, the women try to keep the gardens as neat as they can, but when it does become overgrown, they plant a new one to keep the Earth Mother happy. As they work among the plants, they sing to attract her to their plot of ground and to keep her there.

The Jivaro do not believe in gods, but rather, in spirits, magic, and witchcraft. They think that most illnesses are caused by invisible magic darts that have entered their bodies. The darts, they say, were shot into them by an evil shaman, or sorcerer, and must be removed by a curing shaman.

This curing shaman takes drugs that send him into a trance. Under their influence, he utters strange chants, sees visions, and then proceeds to "suck out" the evil darts and show them to the patient's family. He shows them insects, small plants, or other objects that he claims to have sucked out from the body of the patient, and which represent the evil darts. Actually, he has hidden these objects in his mouth beforehand.

The shamans, both evil and curing, are influential men, and demand high prices for their work. No one wants to antagonize an evil shaman, because he may bewitch him. A curing shaman receives many gifts so that he is willing to give his services when they are needed.

Sometimes, a Jivaro goes to a white doctor living in a village at the edge of the forest. He goes to him if he suffers from a disease such as a severe cold or measles, which were brought by white men, and which therefore a shaman cannot draw out. But now, sometimes he also goes to a white doctor to be treated for stomach pains, dysentery, toothaches and other diseases from which Jivaros suffered before the white men came. For the lives of the Jivaros are changing rapidly.

Changes have been going on among the Jivaros for some years, when missionaries came to the fringe of the jungle to convert them to Christianity. They taught some of the Jivaros living in these border areas to speak Spanish, to read, and to do simple arithmetic. Soon many of the Jivaros discovered how useful these new skills were, especially when they went to work for white settlers. They found they could figure out for themselves how much they were supposed to be paid, and so prevent their employers from cheating them.

The work of the missionaries spread. They built small airstrips to parts of the interior, sent in teachers, and provided medical help. Young Jivaros, eager to learn more about modern life, came to the missionary centers in ever-increasing numbers. They got work with the road-builders that the Ecuador government had sent in to cut through the jungle for cattle-raising settlers. Both the government and the missionaries encouraged the Jivaros, too, to set up small cattle-raising farms.

Missionaries by means of education, and army garrisons stationed at the edge of the jungle, have succeeded in doing away with most of the head-hunting. Laws were passed making it a crime, and some Jivaros have been sent to prison for murder. Although as a result, head-hunting has decreased, it has not been abandoned altogether, for the army cannot, and indeed dare not, send men deep into the jungle to enforce the law.

In 1964, a group of missionaries in the village of Shuar at the edge of the jungle set up an organization called the Jivaro Federation of Shuar Centers. Now the word "Jivaro" has been taken out of the name. Most of the people who come to the centers insist on being called Shuar. The purpose of the Federation is to help keep

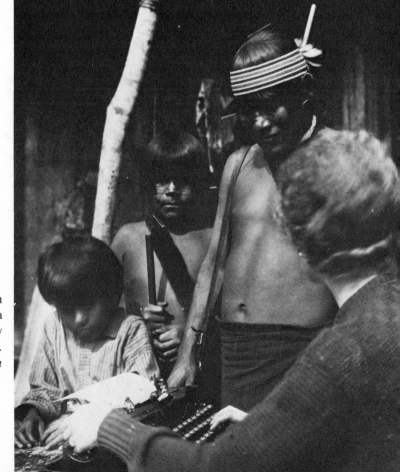

os crowd around an opologist using a writer, a machine they never seen before. um of the American n, Heye Foundation

the good features of Jivaro life, to do away with hatred and revenge-killing, and to offer an education to those who seek it.

At first the Federation Center at Shuar was a simple hut. But enthusiastic young Indians volunteered their labor and have built a large center. In cooperation with the government, there is now a radio broadcasting station, an education center, a health center, and a hostel. Cooperative centers are being formed as well, to sell Jivaro—or Shuar—farm products and handicrafts.

The government does not leave all of the work of modernization to the missionaries. It offers scholarships to bright children who, when they have finished their schooling, go back to their tribes to teach others. It has established health commissions manned by doctors in some of the villages, and offers the people modern health services.

In 1971, an oil company sent prospectors into the jungle to look for oil. As a result, more roads are being built, more Jivaros are being trained to work for the company, and more are learning to read, write, and add. The missionaries have become the protectors of the Jivaros. They even take sides with them against government officials, especially when the officials seem to be in too much of a hurry to change the Jivaros' way of life altogether. By now, the government has come to agree to move only as quickly as the Jivaros themselves want to go toward modernizing their lives.

Many Jivaros find the modern western life style to their liking, and have adopted much of it. They also find that because of better medical care their population is increasing. Numbers of young people are moving out of the jungle to its fringe, to cultivate farms and to raise cattle.

It may be years before those Jivaros who live in the jungle as their fathers and grandfathers did accept any of the white man's ways. Nor can anyone be sure that the government of Ecuador will be able to stamp out completely head-hunting raids and revenge killings. Perhaps, some time in the future, all the Jivaros will finally be convinced that a peaceful life of cooperation with each other is better than one of hatred and distrust. With modern means of communication, with airplanes and helicopters, this time may come sooner than many people expect.

5

The Tiny People of the Forest
The Mbuti Pygmies of Africa

"THE FOREST is our home. When we leave the forest, or when the forest dies, we shall die. We are the people of the forest." So say the tiny people, the Mbuti Pygmies, who live in the Ituri Forest in the northeast corner of the African republic of Zaire.

Where they originally came from, or how they came to live in this great forest in the central part of Africa is a mystery. An inscription in an Egyptian tomb built in 2,500 B.C. shows that they were known to be living in the Ituri forest over four thousand years ago. The inscription tells that the pharaoh buried in the tomb ordered a Pygmy to be brought north, so that he could see for himself one of these tiny people.

The Pygmies are the smallest people in the world, the men about four and a half feet tall, and the women even smaller. Their skin color is reddish-brown, their noses are broad and their lips thin.

Whatever language the Pygmies spoke when they first came to live in the forest has been lost. Now they speak a mixture of three different dialects of Bantu, a language spoken by blacks who live in the central, southern, and eastern parts of the continent. They have picked up the language from contact with the Bantus who live near the edge of the forest, and have adopted it as their own.

The forest is the Pygmies' whole world. They hunt its animals and gather its plants for food. They blend into its lush growth as though they were a very part of it. Their small size and their skin color often make it hard to see them in its dappled shade. They know each kind of plant, whether it can give them food, or a pigment for painting their bodies and their bark cloth. They recognize which vines are best for weaving baskets and belts, which nut or fruit shell can be used to store seeds, or to cook in, or as a paint cup. They can tell, by the way a branch has been bent or broken, which animal has come by and might be hunted.

The Pygmies go about almost completely naked. Living in the forest as they do, clothing would be a hindrance to them. It could catch on bushes and low branches and thus keep them from moving quickly and quietly when hunting. Besides, it rains almost every day, even if only for a short time. Wet clothing would cling uncomfortably to their bodies and chill them, but their bare skin soon dries. The men wear only a loin cloth that is tucked front and back into an intricately woven belt of vines and bark. Loops are made around the belt to hold knives, hatchets, and other tools. Thus, their hands are free to push aside the forest growth as they move through the thick brush.

A bark cloth apron is the only piece of clothing the women wear. They use few ornaments—perhaps some bracelets, anklets, or necklaces of beads, shells, or seeds. Instead of many ornaments, the women and girls paint geometric designs on their bodies. Each one plans her own designs, to suit her tastes, but she usually gets someone to help her apply it. Babies and young children wear nothing at all.

There are about 35,000 Pygmies in the Ituri forest. They live in bands of about six to thirty families, in leaf-covered huts in a forest clearing. A family is made up of a man, his wife, and their children. A few men have two wives. If so, each has her own hut, which is joined to the hut of the other wife, providing the women get along well with each other. Otherwise, the huts are built a few feet apart.

Pygmies consider that a child belongs to the whole band. Although a child knows who his own family is, and sleeps in his mother's hut, he calls every adult "mother," "father," "grandmother," or "grandfather." Children of about the same age call each other "brother" or "sister." When most adults are away at the hunt, those who remain behind look after the children, feed them, scold them if necessary, and play with them.

A band stays in any one camp for about a month. Then, when they have about exhausted the supply of nearby plant foods or the animals are frightened away and hunting becomes poor, one of the older men says it is time to move on. More often, when the camp becomes dirty and smelly because of the piled up refuse, and the leaves covering the huts have dried out, the group abandons the clearing for a new one. They usually have decided in advance where they will make their next camp. It will always be near running water, for the Pygmies love to bathe and splash in the clear streams so plentiful in the Ituri Forest.

On the day of the move, the men tuck their few tools into their belt loops. They tie the nets they use for trapping animals and their other belongings into a bundle. The older boys carry some of the bundles, so that the men can have their hands free to hunt any small game they find as they go to their new camping site.

Every woman has a carrying basket all her own, of closely woven vines. It hangs down her back, and is fastened to a band, a tumpline, that goes around her forehead. If there is any food left she takes it along, but this is not really necessary. Along the way, she will find plenty of mushrooms, roots, and nuts for the next meal.

The most important item every woman takes is a glowing coal from the morning's fire. She wraps it in a large leaf, and carries it all day, until she reaches the new camp. She does not let the coal go out; with a few puffs, she makes it flare up and ignite a few dry leaves and twigs when she wants to build a fire. The Pygmies have no other method of making fire—they get it from something already burning. Probably, they first discovered fire when they saw a tree set aflame by lightning.

Those girls old enough to do so, carry the babies and take care of the small children. This gives the women free hands to gather food, which they drop into their baskets.

And so, talking and singing loudly to warn away animals, the Pygmy band makes its trek to a new clearing. The people are not concerned that the rubbish and huts of their old campground will pollute the forest, for they know that in a very short time a new growth of vegetation will spring up and cover the traces they have left behind.

The band usually reaches its destination long before nightfall. The men arrive first. Each puts his belongings on the spot he has chosen for his hut, and goes off to cut saplings for its construction. When the women arrive, they start building the huts by driving the saplings into the ground close together in the form of a circle six or seven feet wide. Then they bend the thin poles inward, weave the tops together into a lattice, and cover the frame with large leaves. In a short time the small, snug, watertight huts are finished. The women bring their glowing embers inside and light a small fire to take away the damp chill.

Except for some twigs tied to a frame to make a bed, there is nothing else in the hut. Many Pygmies don't even bother with this. They spread out twigs or leaves for sleeping. The huts are so small that very little family activity can take place in them. Most of the time, the people are outside, and retreat into the hut when it rains, or to sleep.

Outside, Pygmies do not sit on the bare ground. Only animals, they say, sit on the ground. They make small tables and chairs of sticks bound together with vines, or they sit on logs, or spread large leaves under their buttocks.

A place is set aside near the stream for the children where they can play without disturbing the adults too much. They splash about in the stream, swing on vines, climb trees, use toy bows and arrows, and play at hunting with small nets. A grandfather often joins them, perhaps pretending to be an antelope caught in the net. The girls make tiny huts and play at keeping house.

The boys play one game they find especially amusing. Six or seven of them climb a sapling, bending it down to the ground. At a signal, all try to leap off at once. Anyone who is too slow goes flying backwards as the young tree snaps upright again. Those who have jumped off in time laugh and jeer at the slowpokes. A boy thus learns to be nimble and quick, as a Pygmy must be in the hunt.

Almost every morning, the camp prepares for the hunt. The men coil their nets into a bundle, take up their spears, bows and arrows, and leave for the hunting ground. The whole camp, except for

Almost hidden by dense forest growth, Pygmy hunters wait patiently for a catch. *American Museum of Natural History*

the very young children and the old people, go along. The women do not carry weapons, but nevertheless play an important part.

At first, the Pygmies walk through the forest in their usual noisy way, chattering, laughing, and singing, to keep away leopards and other animals that they do not hunt. But when they come close to the hunting ground, they become quiet. The men hang the nets from trees and bushes, one next to the other in a semicircle. Sunlight filtering through the leaves makes the mesh hard for the animals to see even from a short distance.

In the meantime, the women and some of the children silently fan out from the nets to complete the circle. Suddenly, they give out great whoops and yells, and bang on the ground with clubs made of rolled-up leaves. They have spotted an antelope and are trying to chase it towards the men. The animal, startled and confused, runs away from the horrifying noise, but is caught in the nets. The men now kill the animal with their spears.

Within a few hours, the band usually has killed enough game for the day. They have also shot a few birds and possibly some monkeys with bows and poisoned arrows.

When they get back to the camp, the food is divided so that everyone in the band gets a share. Special care is taken to see that the old get the tenderest portions, the meat that is easiest to chew. No one goes hungry, even those who, for whatever reason, did not go out to the hunt. The meat is impaled on sticks and roasted over a fire, and mushrooms, nuts and roots wrapped in leaves are cooked in the ashes. Sometimes the women make a stew in a pot that they got by trade with farmers living at the edge of the forest. When no pot is at hand, they use a big leaf curled over.

After the meal, the men start dancing in a circle near the fire. In their dance, they act out the day's events. Soon the women form another circle around the men, and the children join in. The dancing lasts until everyone is tired, and since the day has been very active, it may not be long before the whole camp is sitting around the fire resting.

Evening is story-telling time, singing time, and more dancing time in a Pygmy camp. Pygmies are great storytellers—with many dramatic gestures a man recounts the events of the hunt, sometimes greatly embroidering a tale of prowess, to the amusement of the listeners. Before he has finished, the others start clapping their hands in rhythm, and sing in a chorus. They repeat some of his exploits, in song, and make some additions of their own.

Evening is also the time for planning the next day's hunt. The women are almost sure to have their say, because they want to go where there are plenty of mushrooms and other plants to gather. Around the fire, the decision to move to a new camp is made. And just as important, it is the time for airing grievances and settling disputes.

Since a Pygmy band has no chief, ruling council, or judge, anyone with a complaint against someone else speaks up before the whole group. Those who wish, both men and women, join in the discussion of the rights and wrongs of the situation. Sometimes the argument becomes heated, and voices reach a loud and angry pitch. At this point an older person who has retired to his hut may call out, "I can't sleep, you are making too much noise," or "A noisy camp is a hungry camp. You will frighten away the animals." This has the effect of calming down voices and tempers. It leads to a quick solution that generally satisfies, to some extent, all parties to the dispute.

Crimes are rare among Pygmies. When a person steals or is too lazy to do his share of the work, he is not punished. Instead, he is mocked and laughed at. The other members of the band think his embarrassment punishment enough. Murder and adultery are considered such grave crimes that offenders are banished from the band and condemned to live alone. No other Pygmy band will admit them. The criminals have no protection against dangerous animals and cannot hunt by themselves except to shoot some birds. The punishment meted out to them is almost a sure sentence of death.

Life in a Pygmy camp has its especially joyous time, the honey-gathering days in June and July. When the hives are full, the band breaks up into family groups and each sets out to search for a hive. When the father sees one in the hollow of a tree, he climbs up and thrusts a smoky, slow-burning stick into the hive. Out come the angry, buzzing bees. Even though he is often stung, he pulls out the honeycombs, takes a mouthful of the sweet, sticky stuff, and throws

Pygmy children in the care of an old woman, play near a hut. *American Museum of Natural History*

the combs down to his family. The women and children put them into leaf-covered baskets and carry them back to camp. The honey is shared. There is much merrymaking, dancing, and singing until, tired, they turn in to rest for the next day's honey hunt.

This particular time provides the chance for a family to switch from one band to another. Since there are several bands gathering honey at the same time in the same part of the forest, a family who is unhappy in one group may join the camp of another. The Pygmies think this is better than having quarrels within their group, for the welfare of the band rests on the satisfaction and cooperation of everyone in it.

The Pygmies know that their prosperity depends even more on the forest itself than on harmony within the band. Thus they think the "spirit of the forest" is a benevolent one who looks after them, smiles upon them, and sends them game and plants for food. They do not know what the spirit looks like or where it lives, but feel it must be there, surrounding and protecting them.

This is their only religion. There are no priests and few rituals connected with this religion. However, early in the morning before going on a hunt, the young men take a glowing ember and light a fire under a tree. They say this awakens the forest and warns it, so it will favor the hunt.

At least once a year a band holds a special ceremony, called a *molimo,* for the spirit of the forest. The molimo is performed only at night, and goes on for many nights. This ceremony is usually held at the request of a member of a family in which there has just been a death. Sometimes, if a tragedy has occurred in the band, or if hunting has been very poor, a molimo is called to awaken the spirit of the forest to the plight of its people.

This ceremony gets its name from a trumpet called a molimo, that is blown at that time. It is made of a log that has been hollowed out in a special way. Nowadays some molimo trumpets are made of metal pipes obtained by barter with people living outside the forest.

The men attach much mystery to this trumpet, "give it a drink" in the stream early in the morning before the camp is stirring, hide it by day and take it out at dark. Women and children are forbidden to leave the huts when the molimo is out of its hiding place.

All through the night of the molimo, the trumpet is carried to different parts of the camp, and blown by young men skilled to make it produce eerie sounds. The children huddle, trembling, in the huts, awed and frightened by what they think is the voice of the spirit of the forest. Most of the women know better, for at some time they have managed to get a glimpse of the trumpet.

A Pygmy tribesman calls the spirit of the forest with the molimo. *American Museum of Natural History*

The men add songs and chants to the music from the molimo. The songs do not have many words, just a few ways of saying, "The forest is good," or "The forest is kind." None of the younger men is permitted to doze off during all of this time. Anyone who does is prodded awake, or laughed at. Only the old men are allowed to sleep.

But a time comes when the men realize that being awake so many nights has left them too tired to hunt well, and the band may go hungry. They then carry the trumpet into the forest and hide it until the next time, and the molimo ceremony is ended.

The molimo is the only religious ritual the Pygmies observe. Marriage has no ceremony. When a boy and girl want to get married, the young man first visits the girl's family and asks permission to marry her. This is usually given right away, because the girl has already told her parents that she wants to marry him. But the parents do not consider the youth ready for marriage until he has killed a large antelope and presented it to them, showing he is man enough to take care of a family. When he does this, the girl goes right out and builds a hut for the two of them, and they are considered married.

If the young man is from another band, the couple generally joins his. But wherever they set up housekeeping, it will almost surely be in the Ituri Forest.

Yet many Pygmies do leave the forest for periods of time to work for Bantus and white settlers who cultivate farms at its edge. They also trade forest fruits, honey, animal hides, and meat for iron arrow and spear points, pots, and such foods as bananas, plantains, rice, beans, and flour. But they frighten the farmers with greatly exaggerated stories of the dangers of the forest, to keep them out. They want it to remain as it is, untouched and unspoiled by others.

When working for the farmers, they live in shabby shacks on the rim of the cultivated land, and receive poor wages for their work. With the money they earn, they buy more of the things they cannot get in the forest but have learned to like, such as glass beads, tobacco, and sometimes matches. For the time they adopt quite a few of the customs of the farmers and villagers.

But one day, they feel they have had enough of the hot sun

burning down on them and of the shadeless open farmland. They say they long for the cool quiet of the shadowy forest, with its clear running streams, the chatter of monkeys and the singing of birds. They pack up and slip away, back to their true home, where they are happiest. Here they abandon the customs of the farmers and go back to their own. Months, perhaps a year later, they come back to the village to work once more for the farmers.

At one time the Belgian government, to which Zaire (then called the Belgian Congo) used to belong, tried to bring the Pygmies out of the forest. Clearings were made near its edge and settlements built for them, with schools and health clinics. They were given free tools and seed to start farms. At first, the Pygmies were enthusiastic about the plan, especially about the free things they received. But the plan was doomed to failure, in spite of its good intentions. The Pygmies are not farmers. They ate the seed, sold the tools to the Bantus, and returned to the forest.

Some few left the forest permanently. They were persuaded by both Bantus and whites to set up camps easily reached by road, as a tourist attraction. They charge admission, pose for pictures in clothes they never wore in the forest, go through newly-learned dances, and sell weapons bought from the Bantus. They receive only part of the money they collect, the rest goes to their "bosses." The forest Pygmies scorn these people and call them monkeys. There is little danger that many more Pygmies will join these performers.

Pygmy life is changing nevertheless, for contact with the outside world has not left them altogether untouched. Some are learning to work iron so that they will not be so dependent on the villagers for knives, axes, and spear and arrow points. Some Pygmies have married Bantus and gone to live in the villages, where they find life more to their liking.

But also, the forest is shrinking as more of it is cleared for farming and for road-building. As a result the animals retreat deeper into the forest and the Pygmies follow them. But most of the forest is likely to remain for many years to come, and as long as it does, there will be Pygmies living in it.

6

Boomerang Throwers and Dreamtime People
The Aruntas of Australia

THE HUNTERS of a band of Arunta tribesmen of Australia spy a kangaroo jumping among the bushes. The men divide themselves into two groups. One goes ahead to excite the animal's curiosity about these two-legged creatures. The other sneaks up about twenty feet behind the animal, and the most skillful of the hunters hurls his curved wooden boomerang with great force at the leaping target. His aim is accurate for the animal falls, its belly pierced by the weapon.

The men drag their game back to the camp. They dig a hole big enough to hold the animal, build a roaring wood fire in it, and keep the fire blazing until the hole is covered with about six inches of live coals. Then, holding on to its legs, they heave the animal upside down into the hole. They cover it with more coals from the fire and shovel sand over the coals to keep in the heat.

The animal, its four legs sticking up out of the pit, is roasted for several hours. When it is done the meat is portioned out to everybody in the camp, whether or not a member of the family has taken part in the hunt. As long as there is food, no one is allowed to go hungry.

The Aruntas, or Arandas as they are sometimes called, live in the central part of Australia, in a land of sand and rocks, little rainfall and scanty vegetation. They are one of the tribes of the

Aboriginals, or Aborigines, descendants of the people living in Australia before white men came to settle the continent in 1788. Most scientists think the Aboriginals came to Australia from southeast Asia about 10,000 years ago, in rafts that drifted with the northwest winds.

In appearance, they are different from any other people in the world. The men average about five and a half feet in height, and the women a little less. Their skin is brown and their straight, curly or wavy hair, is dark. Strangely, though, many children are born with blond hair, and remain blond until they become adolescents, then the hair begins to darken.

Aboriginal men have hairy chests and hair on their faces that many allow to grow into beards and mustaches. Both men and women have thin lips and broad noses. Their eyes are deep-set, and topped by ridges that make them look even deeper.

There are very few pure Aboriginals left. Most have mixed with the whites, and adopted many of their ways, yet have kept up some of their tribal life. Among those still living as they probably did thousands of years ago are the Aruntas, a tribe of three or four hundred people.

Central Australia is hot and dry in the summer. Winters are much cooler, the temperature at night sometimes reaching below freezing. Yet all year round the Aruntas wear almost no clothing. What bit they do wear is for decoration rather than protection against the weather. When the women wear anything at all, they put on a very small apron of fur or kangaroo hide. The men sometimes wear a similar apron, but are usually naked except for a belt of human hair from which they hang their few tools. They also often wear strips of kangaroo hide in bands around their foreheads.

Most Arunta men, and some women have a hole drilled through the cartilage between their nostrils. Through this, mainly on ceremonial occasions, they wear a bone which they sometimes decorate with tufts of feathers at each end. For dances and ceremonies they paint geometric designs on their bodies in red, yellow, and white pigments and charcoal. Another type of body decoration is permanent. An Arunta man or woman may have the skin on parts of the body gashed with a sharp stone knife, then have ashes rubbed into the cuts. When the wounds heal, they form raised ridges that the Aruntas consider very ornamental.

The Aruntas are hunters and gatherers. They do not know how to cultivate crops nor raise animals for food. But, as in any other semi-arid region, there is not much wild food to be had at any one time. A large band of people living together in one place would find it almost impossible to get enough food for all to keep alive. Therefore, the Aruntas wander from waterhole to waterhole in small groups of four or five families. Each family is made up of a man, his several wives, and their children.

When they camp, each family builds a crude shelter, hardly more than a lean-to, made by piling brush against poles stuck in the ground. In front of the shelter they build a small fire. They make it by sawing a spear-thrower back and forth against a split stick, and using dried kangaroo dung as tinder.

The fire is the center of family life. Its members cook over it, sit, make their tools, and sleep around it. When nights are cold they huddle together close to it to keep warm.

At dawn each morning, while it is still cool, the camp stirs to life. When the children are fully awake they are given wooden bowls and sent out to fetch water from the nearby waterhole. The filled bowls are passed around and everybody takes a drink. Sipping the water and nibbling at food that has been left over from the day before, the men and women plan their day's activities. The women decide upon the places they will go looking for food, and the men plan the day's hunt.

In two's and three's the women and small children go out to gather food. They take along bowls of drinking water, digging sticks, netted bags, and shallow wooden trays for carrying seeds and berries. The gatherers use the digging sticks to pry out roots, mushrooms, and other fungi. The sticks serve as levers to turn over rocks under which they find caterpillars, beetles, and snakes. Snails, toads, and reptile eggs go into the netted bags. Before the parching sun is high in the sky, they return to the shade of their shelter.

The men and the older boys meanwhile have gone off on their hunt. Perhaps the day before they have found the tracks of an emu, a large flightless ostrich-like bird more than five feet high, that is found only in Australia. It is much sought after because its flesh makes good meat, the strong leg tendons make sturdy cords, and its feathers are used for decoration.

To hunt the emu, they take along a spear-thrower and a slender spear about nine feet long. The spear-thrower is a two or three-foot long leaf-shaped piece of wood slightly hollowed out along its length, with a wooden hook near one end. The spear has a hole at the blunt end. When it is to be thrown, it is placed on the thrower and attached loosely to the hook, through the hole. With a backhand motion the hunter thrusts the spear-thrower forward without letting go of it, and the spear flies out with great force.

For the actual hunt the Aruntas build a blind made of branches near the bed of a dry creek. They dig a hole in the creek bed so that water seeps in from below and then hide in the blind, hoping the bird will come to drink. They wait patiently and silently, barely moving, until the emu appears and gets close. Then one of the men slides a spear into his spear-thrower and hurls the weapon. A good shot kills the bird, but if the spear misses, there is no second chance. The bird has been frightened and runs away on its fast legs. The men must content themselves with a few lizards they can catch by digging them out of their burrows and hitting them over the head with sticks.

For hunting kangaroos and wallabies, the Aruntas use a boomerang. This is a piece of curved heavy wood two to three feet long. When thrown with force, it is a powerful weapon that can cut open an animal's abdomen.

The boomerang used by the Aruntas and other Aboriginals is not made to return to its thrower if it misses, as many people believe. The returning boomerang is used mainly in sports and is sold to tourists, some of whom think they are getting an authentic Aboriginal weapon. In fact, most returning boomerangs are nowadays made of plastic, many manufactured in the United States and sent to Australia.

In hunting birds, a boomerang has a unique use. The Aruntas spread nets between low trees or bushes, and hide. When a flock of

Opposite: An Arunta hunter stands poised for the kill. He uses the spear-thrower for large game. *American Museum of Natural History*

birds flies close, the hunters throw the boomerang at the flock and because of its shape, it sails through the air in a curved path. They say the birds think the boomerang looks like an eagle or a hawk swooping down on the flock. The birds panic, become confused, change their course, and fall into the nets.

Some of the plants brought back to the camp are eaten raw. The Aruntas do not know how to make pottery, and have no cooking utensils of any kind. Cooked foods are baked or roasted in hot ashes or on flat stones. Some of the seeds and roots are crushed on grinding stones and baked into cakes that can be kept for days without spoiling.

There is no set mealtime. When the food is ready, the people sit on the ground and eat it. Since animals are roasted whole, small ones are often overcooked, and large ones are rare, almost raw. The large animals—wallabies, kangaroos, and emus, are not successfully hunted very often, so one is a treat. Most of the meat the Aruntas get consists of various kinds of lizards. More than half of all the food they eat are plants gathered by the women and children.

The little children stay close to the women. A child's mother, his aunts, and grandmothers all help to take care of it. Sometimes an aunt suckles a baby if its mother cannot or is too busy to do so at the time. Everybody in the camp pets and spoils the children. They are given a great deal of freedom, and seldom scolded or struck. But if a child at any time becomes a nuisance by continually hitting someone, or goes into a temper tantrum, he may expect some hard smacks from any adult in the band.

In the hottest part of the day everybody rests or naps in the shade. As it gets cooler, the people start their various tasks. The women grind more of the seeds and fruit they have gathered and bake them into cakes, and string net bags from plant fibers. The girls look on and imitate their mothers, using bits of string they find around the camp.

The boys watch their fathers and learn how to chip stones into scrapers and knives, and attach resin or wood to the tool as a handle. If new ones are needed the men make spears from the tough wood of the ironwood tree, using stone tools to cut the shaft to the desired size and shape. They make sure their boomerangs and especially their spear-throwers are in good condition, for these are among their most useful implements.

Besides their use in hunting and firemaking, the spear-throwers are used as trays for mixing pigments for body painting for religious ceremonies. They are also used as instruments for tapping out rhythms, and as very efficient woodworking tools if a stone flake is attached to one end.

Both boomerangs and spear-throwers are used as shovels for clearing thorns and pebbles from campsites. The boomerang is a butchering tool and a fighting stick. Two of them, tapped together, become rhythm sticks. Because the Aruntas have no beasts of burden, they carry very few tools from camp to camp, and so each tool has to have many uses.

A man's total possessions weigh about 21 pounds, and a woman's about 12. They seldom take all of their stone tools with them when they change camps. Instead, they make new ones as they need them. The women leave behind their heavy grinding stones to use again when they return to the site, for they know no one will take them. As is true of most desert people, anyone coming upon someone's tools leaves them for the rightful owner.

The Arunta band has no leader or chief but the older people are consulted when a move is being considered or a dispute arises, and their opinion is respected. When starting a move, the men tuck their flint knives and the small bark pouches in which they keep pigments for body painting into their belts. They pick up their spears, spear-throwers, boomerangs, their sacred objects, and are ready to go. The women carry their net bags, trays, digging sticks, and babies in soft bark cradles, and the trek to another, fuller water hole starts. They move in this way in a well-known circuit and each season return to a campsite they occupied once before.

During this trek, they meet other bands, exchange information about relatives, and often arrange marriages. Arranging a marriage is not a simple matter, because the rules that govern which two people may marry are very complicated, probably more so than anywhere else in the world. They stem from the way the whole Arunta social structure is set up.

The Arunta society is divided into two main groups. No one

knows for certain how the division was first made, but the Aruntas say it has been there since they themselves came into being. Each of these groups is divided into two sub-groups, and these in turn into two sections. A boy belongs to his father's main group and sub-group and a girl to her mother's. But a child's section is different from that of either parent. It is determined, in a traditional way, by which section each parent belongs to. The system is very difficult for an outsider to understand, but the Aruntas from earliest childhood know just where they belong.

Two people from the same section may not marry, and the rule is very strict about this. There is yet another complication. In childhood, a boy and girl are betrothed but not in expectation of marrying each other. As a symbol of betrothal the girl promises to make the boy a belt woven from her own hair. The girl, when she is eleven or twelve years old, is married to a man of the proper section who was betrothed to her mother in *her* childhood. The girl's daughter by this older man becomes the wife of the one she was betrothed to. Complicated? Yes indeed! But in this way a man is certain that he will have at least one wife young enough to gather food for him in his old age.

The betrothal and marriage arrangements have an advantage for the girl too. She will be provided for if anything happens to prevent her parents from doing so. She herself feels secure in the protection that a marriage to an older man and an experienced hunter can give her. A girl is not forced to marry a man to whom she has been promised, but she rarely refuses. If she does, her parents arrange for another marriage that suits her better.

The wedding ceremony itself is much simpler. The men assemble in one part of the camp and decorate the groom with paint and feathers. Meanwhile, the young bride may be sitting on her mother's lap. The bridegroom comes to his future mother-in-law, to whom he was once betrothed, and says, "Give me your daughter." He then takes the girl by the arm, and she pretends to resist. The mother puts the girl's arm into the man's hand and he squeezes it. This is considered a sign that they are married, and the girl usually goes to live with her new husband's family and with any other wives he has.

After the marriage, the groom is not allowed to speak to his

A tribal elder. Unlike the Ik, the Arunta honor their older tribesmen. *Australian News and Information Bureau*

mother-in-law again, except during big tribal ceremonies, when the rule is often overlooked.

If a woman becomes a widow, she most likely will marry again, for in addition to a young wife most men want an older one. They say an older wife is not likely to be dissatisfied or chase after other men. Sometimes two or three old widows live together in a single hut, and a few old widowers in another. Neither group wants to get married again, but they help provide food for each other when they can. In any event, sons and daughters always make sure their elderly parents do not lack for food.

Right after the heavy summer rains of February and March, there is an abundance of water and game. The Arunta bands take advantage of this and wander to areas far from their usual grounds. This makes it possible for them to get together with other bands for as long a period of time as there is enough food and water for a large group. There may be as many as 150 people camping in one place. This is the best time for arranging marriages, and for large religious ceremonies.

While the bands are together, there is much singing and dancing, accompanied by the only musical instruments the Aruntas
know—sticks or boomerangs hit together, and sticks tapped against
spear-throwers to beat out rhythm. During that time, too, some of
the boys between the ages of 10 and 12 are initiated into manhood.
First, the boys stand in a group in the clearing. The men gather
around them, and two or three of the men toss each boy into the air
several times. Other men catch the boys as they fall. All this time
the women dance around the men and boys, swinging their arms and
shouting. This part of the ceremony symbolizes that the boys have
become free from their mothers.

Their bodies decorated with geometric designs, young Aboriginals perform
a tribal dance. *Australian News and Information Bureau*

Now they must associate with men and avoid women. The boys are segregated in the bush, away from the main group. They live there, alone, except for visits from the men. A boy's grandfather or father pierces the soft cartilage between his nostrils and inserts a bone, which he may now wear whenever he wishes.

While they are living in the bush, the men introduce them to the secret rituals of the tribe. The boys are sworn never to reveal to the women, girls, and uninitiated boys what they have learned.

A few days after the tossing-up ceremony the boys undergo several painful physical ordeals, which they try to bear silently without any show of fear lest they be thought unworthy of manhood. The last of these is the scalp-biting ceremony. The boys sit on the ground, the men surround them, and bite the boys' scalps until the blood flows freely. They say this will make the hair grow strong. Now the boys may return to the whole group, and are considered adults.

The Arunta's religion is based on the belief that there was, in the distant past, a Dreamtime, when animal spirits existed before the Aboriginals themselves did. In this Dreamtime, the spirit creatures traveled from place to place across the desert, and created the plants, animals, and men now found there. Most of the dances performed during religious ceremonies represent these spirit creatures of the Dreamtime and their work of creation. The women have no part in the religious life.

Besides being part of a group, a sub-group, and a section, every Arunta is a member of a clan thought to be descended from a certain animal, plant or other natural object which is the clan's *totem*. The totem has a spirit which is so sacred that members of its clan are strictly forbidden to eat that particular plant or animal.

A child does not automatically become a part of his father's totem-clan, since the Aruntas do not consider him his real father. They do not understand that a man's sperm must fertilize the woman's egg before a child can be born. They think the man prepares the woman's body for the entrance of the totem-spirit, who is the real father of the child. When a baby is born the older men of the band question the mother closely about the place where she thinks the child was conceived. From her answers they determine which totem-spirit was near at that time, and decide that this totem-spirit is the child's father. The child is then assigned to that totem-clan. If, for example, the mother thinks the child was conceived near some emu tracks, the child becomes a member of the emu totem-clan; if she saw a lizard running in the sand, he is put into the lizard clan. Thus a child's totem-clan may not necessarily be the same as his father's.

Each totem-clan has a sacred object called a *churinga,* that represents its totem-spirit. It is kept well hidden in a cave, hollow tree, or a cache in a special area set aside for it some distance away from the camp. Churingas are sometimes made of wood, but more usually of stone. They are flat, oval slabs painted with designs of concentric circles, dots, spirals, and animal tracks. They are so sacred that only males initiated into the totem-clan may view them or come near the place where they are kept. When the band moves on, each churinga is covered and carried by one of the men in its totem-clan.

During some religious ceremonies certain wooden churingas are used as *bullroarers.* These churingas have a hole drilled through one end, and a string of human hair passed through it. The bullroarer is twirled rapidly through the air, and as it spins, gives off a loud, eery roaring noise supposed to be the voice of its totem-spirit. It is a chilling sound, frightening all but the initiated males.

Aruntas think illness and death are caused by magic spells cast upon the victim by an evil person. The spell is cast by pointing certain objects in the direction of the victim's camp and chanting a curse such as "May your heart be rent asunder" or "May your backbone be split and your ribs torn out." The object used may be a long, narrow double-pointed board carved with magical symbols, a sharp engraved bone, or a large piece of pointed stone soft enough to have designs cut into it. These pointers are considered so potent that a man using one is careful not to have it point to his relatives or friends lest they be affected by it.

When a person becomes sick, a shaman or sorcerer is called upon to counteract the evil spell. He takes out a bundle of small objects which he believes have magical powers. Among them are usually glassy stones, quartz crystals, and snail shells, which are spread out and a chant intoned over them. If the patient does not re-

A churinga, or carved sacred stone, used in religious ceremonies. *Australian News and Information Bureau*

cover then the spell is thought to be too powerful to be overcome by any means.

Sometimes the dying person whispers to the shaman the name of the one he thinks has cast the spell upon him. If he does not, the shaman investigates who might have done so. It may take him two or three years to decide who the culprit is. He then uses his pointer to cast a spell upon this victim. The cursed person is supposed to be stricken in about one month, unless his life is saved by his own shaman.

Before too many years have passed, the Aruntas will probably learn different ways to treat diseases. For they are occasionally visited by anthropologists who come to study their culture, and by other Aboriginals who have had a great deal of contact with white Australians. From them, they hear about the outside world.

These other Aboriginals usually come from tribes who abandoned their nomadic life and live near white Australian settlements. They work for the white settlers, live in shacks instead of crude shelters, get water from wells, wear western type clothing and eat some western type foods. When they get sick, they often go to the doctors in health clinics or in the settlements for help.

People from these tribes also went into cities to look for work. They found that they had few skills needed to get jobs, and even when they did have some skills, were often discriminated against because they were Aboriginals. Finally, they joined together to exert pressure on the Australian government to outlaw discrimination, and grant more money for health and education than had been allowed so far. They also pressed for the right to have a hand in making and carrying out plans to integrate Aboriginals into white Australian culture. But in addition, they wanted to work out ways to preserve some of their own tribal customs and language so that these would not be lost forever.

The Australian government has taken a number of steps to fill these needs. The most important was the passing of laws barring discrimination against all minorities in jobs, housing, and other social matters. And, in recognitition of the place Aboriginals hold in Australian life, July 13, 1973 was proclaimed National Aboriginal Day. In November of that year a committee called the National

Aboriginal Consultative Committee was elected by the Aboriginals themselves. Every Aboriginal, no matter where he lived, was eligible and urged to vote, and about 40,000 did so.

The Committee advises the government on all matters concerning Aboriginals. With government money, it has set up a radio station from which programs are broadcast both in English and in the Aboriginal languages. It publishes a magazine called IDENTITY, in which Aboriginal problems are discussed and suggestions for their solution welcomed. But it cannot enforce any of the laws against discrimination; it can only bring cases of such lawbreaking to the attention of the authorities.

Most of the Committee's work reaches those Aboriginals who live in cities, near white settlements or government stations. The few nomadic tribes such as the Aruntas are too far removed from these centers to feel any of its effects. Slowly, however, news will filter in to them of how other Aboriginals are living. They will learn much more than the little bit they know about settled life on farms, sheep stations and towns. In time the Aruntas may send their children to schools in centers away from the tribal grounds. Most of these young people will probably never want to return to nomadic life, but will go to work on farms or in cities. If this happens, as it well may, the Aruntas will eventually disappear as a nomadic tribe. But the Committee will do its best to help the Aruntas gather together to speak their own language and to practice those of their old rituals they wish to keep.

Two Onge tribesmen with elaborate, everyday face and body paint. *Lido Cipriani*

7

The Jungle Negritos
The Onges of
Little Andaman Island

WITHOUT EVER having seen a single one, Marco Polo, the Italian traveler of the thirteenth century, wrote that the Negritos of the Andaman Islands kill and eat any stranger they capture. He had heard this from others, who had never met any Negritos either. This rumor stemmed from the accounts of two Arabs who visited the islands in the year 871, and who said that the people living there were cannibals. Stories about these fierce man-eaters persisted for almost a thousand years. Seafarers, in fear of their lives, avoided this group of jungle-covered islands in the Bay of Bengal about 200 miles southwest of Burma.

But the British needed a naval base in the islands to replenish their ships' supplies of fresh food and water. In 1858, in spite of the hostility of the native people, they succeeded in setting up a well-protected colony on Great Andaman Island, the largest of the group. It was many years before the natives came to tolerate the intruders. In those years, the British discovered that the Andamanese, although savagely warlike where outsiders were concerned, were generally peaceful among themselves. True, they hacked captives to pieces, but did not cook and eat them, as had been reported.

The Andaman Islands now are part of India. The "little negroes"—the Negritos who inhabit them, are less than five feet tall, although not quite so small as the African Pygmies. Almost all are still Stone Age people, with no knowledge of how to smelt iron or any other metal. Some of those living on Great Andaman Island have had contact with whites and government agents from India, and have learned to use iron knives, axes, and other such tools.

However, among the Onges, the Negritos of Little Andaman Island, most do not know how to make even stone tools, only those of wood or shell. Neither do they know how to produce fire. They probably first found fire in the forest, and preserved it by kindling one from another. The Onges are for the most part living as men did even before the Stone Age. About 700 Onges are known to be on Little Andaman Island. Most of them live along the shore, and those that are inland are near a stream or saltwater inlet of the sea.

All year round the weather is warm, sometimes hot and moist. In this warm climate there is no need for clothing as protection against cold, and the Onges wear very little or none. The young children are naked, the men and older boys sometimes wear loin cloths, the women and girls have very short bushy aprons made of plant fibers in front.

Both men and women wear short necklaces of wild pig tusks, shells, seeds, and strips of bark. They also take great pleasure in making flower garlands to wear around their necks and arms. One kind of necklace is made from the ribs and small bones of the feet and hands of dead members of their families. For special ceremonies and feasts they hang the jawbones of ancestors around their necks. This is not done in disrespect for the dead, but to appease their spirits, so that the wearer will come to no harm from them.

For decoration, Onge men and women use white clay and several shades of ochre to paint each other's faces and bodies in elaborate geometric designs. Because they believe they may become sick and die if the paint is not renewed very frequently, the face, at least, is done afresh almost every day. One way a wife shows her love for her husband is by the fancy lines and curves with which she paints him. None of the Onges' designs have any special meaning, but they are striking in appearance against their almost black skins.

The lack of hair on the negritos' faces and bodies make it unnecessary for them to shave. But both men and women shave all around the edge of their hair. The actual process of shaving is done

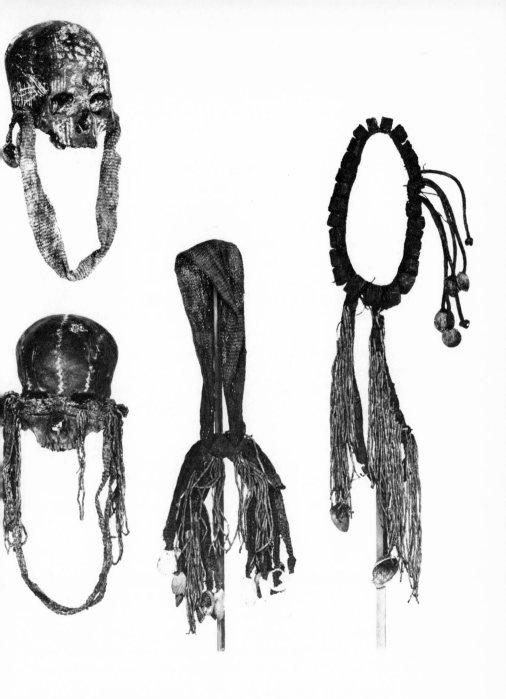

Human skull and bone necklaces worn to appease ancestral spirits. *American Museum of Natural History*

by women, rarely by men. For razors, they use sharp-edged splinters of stone which they knock off from a large chunk, but do not shape in any other way. They do not take the trouble to sharpen any of the stone razors when they become blunt, but simply throw them away. This is the only stone tool they use. When they find bottles that have been cast up on shore, they break them and use the sharp glass for shaving.

The sea also washes in pieces of iron from wrecked ships, which the Onges sharpen against a stone, attach to a wooden handle, and use as a hatchet. Some of it they break and hammer with a rock into arrow points.

Sometimes an empty oil drum floats to shore. The Onges cut it in half, use each part as a cooking pot, and when the iron rusts away, the pot is discarded. They make no pots of their own.

An Onge village consists of eight to twelve families all living together in one communal hut. The hut is built near a fresh water source such as a spring. The men construct a large beehive-shaped framework on poles, sometimes as much as 60 feet across at the ground level. This done, they help the women collect large quantities of palm leaves, and then consider their part in the house-building finished. The women weave the leaves in overlapping layers into waterproof mats with which they cover the frame almost completely. They leave some space all around between the wall and the ground. One end of the palm-mat covering is left as a flap that can be lifted up and used for a door.

But in such a large hut, it is often more convenient to go in or out by crawling through the space under the wall than by using the door. Through it, too, trash, sweepings, and garbage are pushed out and a ring of dirt accumulates around the hut. It does not bother the Onges, for when they do not want to use the main door they crawl through this dirt.

The hut may last as long as ten years, if it is repaired as needed. However, in time termites weaken the wooden framework or the roof mats can no longer be mended. Then the hut is knocked down, the floor cleared, and the ring of trash is leveled off for the floor of a new dwelling.

Inside the hut, each family marks off its section by lengths of wood laid on the floor. A large bambo platform built close to the wall and covered with a mat is the family bed. The man, his wife and children, with heads toward the center where the roof is highest, sleep on the one bed. The middle of the hut is left clear for cooking in the rainy season.

Family possessions are kept in small closely woven baskets, about five inches across and six inches deep, shaped like half an egg. They hold little crab-claw pipes that the men use to smoke a certain aromatic leaf; spiral nautilus-shell drinking cups, necklaces, and anything else the family members want to keep in the hut. The baskets are highly prized and are handed down from mother to daughter until they finally break.

Each man has one wife, who may be from either his own group or from any other on the island. Families are small, with two or three children. The parents show great love and gentleness not only to their own children but to any others. Very often a man and wife lend a child to another couple as a sign of friendship, especially if the couple is childless. The "adopted" child may remain for years with his new parents, sometimes permanently. He knows who his real parents are, and thinks of himself as having two mothers and fathers.

The people living in the hut choose a leader from among themselves, a man they consider wise and just. He has no authority over the others, but is asked for advice and to help settle disputes that may arise. All final decisions about the activities of the group are made democratically. If a person has committed a crime such as stealing, the group as a whole decides whether the offender deserves banishment. This sentence is almost never invoked, and crime of any kind, simple or serious, is extremely rare.

The Onges lead an easy life. Food is plentiful near the communal hut, and in a few hours the women can gather what the family needs. What they cannot reach by hand they bring down from the trees with a hooked pole that they keep in the forest for this purpose. They use a sharp digging stick to get roots out of the ground, sometimes digging up a yam as big as a football.

Anything a woman gathers she puts into a basket which, supported by a band around her head, hangs down her back. These carrying baskets are different from those used for storage. They are carelessly made and not meant to last. When they are emptied of the things that have been brought back to the camp, they are usually discarded. There are small ones for the children and bigger ones of various sizes for the adults.

When the season comes for the ripening of certain fruits that grow a distance away, the group leaves the big hut and goes off to gather them. Here each family builds its own temporary shelter, hardly more than a lean-to with a sloping leaf-covered roof, built quickly wherever there is a supply of leaves. The men, women and children join in gathering the food. As soon as the particular fruit season is over, they go back to the communal hut.

The plant foods furnish only part of the Onges' diet. Wild pigs abound in the jungle, and the men, with their dogs, go out in small bands to hunt them with bows and arrows, or spears. The arrow and spear points are of shell or iron, if any has been found on shore. The Onges began using dogs in hunting after the early 1900's, when out-siders brought the animals to the island. They soon discovered that the dogs were able to track down wild pigs and hold them at bay for the hunter to shoot or spear. Now each family owns several dogs, and many more run wild on the island.

Wild pigs are about the only land animals the Onges hunt. They collect the cocoons of cicadas and the large white larvae of certain grasshoppers, and roast them. However, their most plentiful animal food comes from the sea.

The women stand in shallow water close to the shore and catch small fish and crabs in nets. They also net fish in rivers and marshes. The men do most of the fishing. They wade out to the coral reefs, and shoot fish, crabs, and giant crayfish with bows and arrows and harpoons, some of which they tip with iron.

The harpoon is a spear-like arrow shot from a bow, but unlike an arrow, it has a detachable barbed point which is held to the shaft by a cord. When the harpoon is shot off, the point becomes sepa-rated from the shaft and remains embedded in the victim.

Since big fish, turtles, and other sea animals are found in deeper water, the Onges go out in canoes to shoot or harpoon them.

Opposite: A mother feeds her baby from a Nautilus shell. *Lidio Cipriani*

Tribesman spearing a turtle. *American Museum of Natural History*

If they are lucky they catch a dugong, a strange fish-like mammal that lives in the Indian Ocean and its seas and is much sought after for its fine taste.

Giant turtles are a valuable food supply. The men hunt them from their canoes at night, when the reptiles are fairly close to land. They never kill a turtle on the shore at night because they believe its spirit walks there in the dark. On the water, they feel safe from any evil the turtle's spirit may wish to cause them, since the spirit does not leave the shore.

Mornings, the men search the soft sand for footprints of turtles. These lead them to clusters of leathery eggs the size of billiard balls, that the females have buried in the sand during the night. The men fill many baskets with the eggs, for they are considered a great delicacy.

The canoes are the only means of transportation the Onges have, and therefore take great pains in making them. Sometimes a man works alone, but usually all the men in the settlement help in the construction of a canoe. By agreement, when it is finished it belongs only to the one man. It is hollowed out from the trunk of a softwood tree which has been laboriously felled, usually with a wooden ax. A few Onges have been able to get iron axes from anthropologists and missionaries who have visited them, and this considerably lightens the work of cutting down the tree.

Then, with blades of shell or washed-up iron, the men gouge out the inside of the log. The bow and stern are alike. They construct a platform on each end, on which harpooners stand to sight their prey and to cast their barbs. Outrigger poles attached to one side of the boat helps balance it in rough water. As a last touch, the women paint designs on the outside of the boat. Although the paint will begin to wash off at its first launching, the canoe is not painted again.

The canoes are never left in the water when they are not in use, because they are too fragile to withstand the pounding of the surf. After each fishing expedition they are dragged up on land near the communal hut and by means of rollers launched again when needed.

The Onges who do not live along the shore make canoes in the same way. They use them on the inland waters for fishing, as the shore people do, and to take them down the streams to the sea.

In mid-March, when the honey in the hives is at its peak, the Onges go into the forest for the sweet, golden-colored jellylike liquid. The families walk in single file, men first, for the jungle is always so dense that it is almost impossible to travel it in any other way.

When a man finds a hive, he puts his mark on the tree as a sign of ownership, and no one else will take the hive. Stealing another's honey tree is considered such a serious crime that its punishment is banishment from the band, and therefore almost certain death.

Once he has established ownership, the man picks a handful of leaves of a certain plant, chews it to a pulp and smears the pulp over his body. The leaves are odorless to humans, but apparently give off a smell that bees can sense, for it repels them and the honey-gatherer is never stung. As he climbs the tree, he chews more of the leaves and spits them at the bees as they fly out of the hive, to keep them from attacking the bystanders.

When he brings down the hive and it is opened, he dips a long

The Onges perform a ceremonial dance that represents meeting and parting. *American Museum of Natural History*

strip of bark into the honey. Everybody takes turns biting off a piece of the sweetened bark and licking it. What is not eaten then and there is brought back in wooden buckets made from hollowed-out logs.

During the honey-gathering season, as for some of the great pig hunts, a number of groups band together for mutual help and for feasting. Whatever is hunted or gathered is divided evenly. If there is a dispute, the differences are soon settled, and apologies may go on for days, each party assuring the others that no insult was intended.

The feasting lasts for a week or more, and vast quantities of honey, fish, and pork are consumed. Dancing goes on in shifts throughout the days and nights. The men bend their legs back and slap their calves against their buttocks in rhythm, while the women clap their hands, then slap one thigh. All the while both the men and women sing. The Onges have no musical instruments of any kind, but they get the rhythm for the dancing by this slapping.

Because these feasts are special occasions, there is even more body painting than usual. Human bone necklaces and jawbones of ancestors as well as shell ornaments hang around the necks of the men and bounce with the dancing.

The time comes when the feasters are tired, and bloated with too much food. Then the dancing breaks off, and each group walks back through the jungle to its own communal hut. For days afterwards, they eat only vegetables and fruits, until the ill effects of overeating are gone.

If a person becomes sick, whether from stuffing himself with food or from any other cause, the whole community helps care for the family and provides it with food. To reduce fever, the patient's whole body is smeared with a mixture of ochre, turtle fat, and honey, and his legs, arms, chest, and abdomen are bound tightly with strips of bark. Generally the fever subsides, as it probably would anyway. The Onges have no other way of treating illness.

There are no medicine men, prayers, or religious ceremonies to help cure the sick. In fact, there are no religious ceremonies of any kind. The Onges believe, however, that there is a supreme being who takes the shape of a lizard bigger than a crocodile. This being

A woman, her legs bound tightly with strips of bark, undergoes a tribal method of curing illness. *Lidio Cipriani*

lives in the sky; thunder is his voice, and the wind his breath. If he is angry, he breathes out storms and throws burning tree trunks down to earth. The Onges do not love this being. Rather, they fear him, yet do not perform any rituals to appease him.

They do fear the spirits of their ancestors, and never wish to make them angry. They bury a dead person under the family bed so that the spirit will feel it is respected, and thus will not desert them. A few months later they dig up the body, take certain of the bones, particularly the jawbone, for necklaces, to show the spirit that it is not being cast out from among them.

But they believe that the spirits of dead enemies can bring them harm. In order to drive away these spirits, they burn the bones and thus force the spirits out. The charred human bones found by early European visitors to Little Andaman Island probably gave rise to the rumor that its inhabitants are cannibals.

In more than a hundred years since first the British and then the Indians came to stay in the Andaman Islands, there has been very little change in the life of the Onges. There are still only a few outsiders who come to Little Andaman Island. The Onges' tools are not much different from the way they have been for perhaps thousands of years, except for some iron axes they have received from these visitors. One anthropologist who lived with the Onges for two years gave them fishhooks and lines, and showed them their use, but the people do not like them. They prefer their own way of fishing.

Yet the Onges are eager to have their illnesses treated by what they consider the magic of western medicine, but there is not much of it available on Little Andaman Island.

The Indian government has made some attempts to set up plantations of coconuts, papayas, yams, and tapioca to introduce new foods to the Onges, but the people do not want to cultivate them. They have no need to, for the jungle and the sea give them everything they want for food.

In this age of jet planes and easy travel, sooner or later tourists will "discover" Little Andaman Island. When they do, they will undoubtedly introduce new things and ideas to its people. No one knows as yet whether the Onges will accept or reject them as they did the fishhooks the anthropologist gave them.

8

From Cannibalism to Self-Government

The People of Papua — New Guinea

WITH blood-chilling shouts and war cries, thousands of gaudily painted tribesmen wearing head-dresses of brilliant bird-of-paradise feathers charge down the field, brandishing long wooden spears. Another tribe in different but equally brilliant paint and feathers advances toward them. Before the two meet head-on, the second mob turns and retreats, the first following wildly. Soon the action is reversed and the pursuer becomes the pursued. Over and over again the roles of the groups change, but each time the first attackers gain a few yards toward an open field about half a mile away.

A battle that took place a few years earlier is being acted out, this time as a ceremony, not a real fight.

Crowds of people from villages many miles around stand along the sides of the field and watch. In the crush they trample the sweet potato vines that are planted in neat patches in the fields. The display goes on for hours, and except by accident, no one, spectator or participant, is hurt.

Finally the two opposing sides reach the field agreed upon earlier as the place for the conclusion of the "battle." Here the "winning" tribe pays the other a sum of Australian money and a number of pigs. This represents compensation for the killing of several men in a past battle. Acting out the battle scenes is part of the ceremony of compensation or *payback*. Although the tribes still consider themselves enemies, peace has been made even though it may only last a year or two. Pig-roasting, feasting and dancing follow and continue all night long.

Once, here in the highlands of Papua-New Guinea, when a tribesman had been killed, a revenge-killing raid was the custom. Thus there was constant warfare between the tribes. The people were among the most fearsome and feared in the world. Now such raids are rare. Instead, the elders of both tribes bargain and agree upon compensation in the form of money, pigs, and native birds called cassowaries.

The island of New Guinea is about 90 miles north of Australia, in the Pacific Ocean. It is the second largest island in the world, next to Greenland. The western half, West Irian, is part of Indonesia. The eastern half is Papua-New Guinea, a United Nations trust territory under Australian control.

Along the coasts and rivers the land is a tropical jungle, hot and humid, but the interior is mountainous and the climate pleasant. Jagged peaks pierce the horizon, some rising to heights of over 12,000 feet. Because there is a great deal of rain in season, the steep mountainsides are covered with heavy vegetation. Fertile valleys watered by swiftly running streams cut through the mountains. Here, surrounded by trees, the cane called pit-pit, and the tall kunai grass are the villages of thatched huts of the people of the Highlands.

The Highlanders were the last inhabitants of New Guinea to be discovered. There probably are still some groups in remote regions who have never seen a white man or who have had no contact with western culture.

In the early 16th century European explorers came to the coast of New Guinea and many years later missionaries and traders went a short way up the wide rivers that empty into the sea. They found Stone Age people who grew most of their food in small gardens, fished, and hunted crocodiles which they were willing to trade for cloth, beads and other goods. But they were also fierce cannibals, constantly at war with each other, head-hunting for revenge, prestige, as a show of manhood, and sometimes to get meat. White

Tribesmen in full battle array charge down a field as part of the payback ceremony. *Rebecca B. Marcus*

settlers and missionaries dared not go into the mountainous interior, where, if attacked, escape was almost impossible. In fact, they thought there could hardly be any people living there because the mountains seemed impenetrable.

In 1928, however, rumors of gold in the stream beds brought a few bold prospectors to the fringes of the Highlands. They learned that the interior was indeed inhabited, and by tribes as warlike and cannibalistic as those along the coasts and rivers. For the next few years men in small low-flying planes were surprised to see many villages and neat vegetable gardens dotting the deep valleys.

The valleys appeared to have the right conditions for growing coffee and other profitable crops. To explore the possibilities of the land, a group of Australians built an airstrip in the Highlands in the middle 1930's. They set up small coffee plantations and hired native New Guineans to work for them. A few white settlements sprang up in the Highlands, and some Highlanders came to work there. The outbreak of World War II stopped further development except that Allied forces built a few roads inland from the coast.

The Australian government later extended the roads and hired Highlanders to help with the work. With the money these men earned they began to buy goods such as pots, cloth, body paint, steel knives and axes, and matches, in trade stores set up by enterprising Australians.

There are now several roads cutting through the valleys and connecting the towns that have been established by Australians. Trucks bring goods from the coast to the trade stores. There are small passenger buses running infrequently between towns, and a small airline carrying both cargo and passengers. In spite of these changes, many of the villages can still only be reached on foot.

Australia also set up some schools and health centers to introduce western education and health practices to the people of Papua-New Guinea. Unlike some other Stone Age tribes that have remained isolated, many Highlanders have access to the goods and ideas of western civilization. For instance, it is possible to see tribesmen in full ceremonial dress of paint, shells and feathers waiting in an airport for a flight. But except for those living in or near big towns, most Highlanders choose to cling to the way of life their people have been leading for centuries. They remain in their villages, occasionally coming in to a trade store to sell firewood, handicrafts, and crops they grow, and to buy a few things they want to take back with them.

The villages they live in hold anywhere from about 40 people to several hundred. In some, the houses are circular, like beehives, but most are rectangular. They are built of a framework of poles, between which are stretched mats woven of palm, and thatched with palm or pandanus leaves, or kunai grass.

The Highlanders, like all the people of New Guinea, have dark brown, almost black skins. Hair grows on the men's chests and faces, but many shave their faces with razors of sharpened bamboo slivers, or pull the hair out with tweezers made from two small pieces of bamboo.

Most of the tribesmen circle their waists with a belt woven of plant fiber. From this they hang a bark apron or loincloth in front and a bunch of big, broad leaves in the back. The women wear fringed grass aprons front and back, and the children are usually naked. In some tribes men wear a wrap-around bark cloth or cotton skirt called a lap-lap.

A woman's dress is not complete without her *bilum*. This is a big mesh bag netted of plant fibers, with a long straplike loop across its open end. She puts the loop around her head and lets the bilum hang down her back. In it she puts anything she would have to carry in her hands—sweet potatoes and taro roots she digs up, balls of fiber cord, grass for her skirt. If she has a baby she makes a bed of leaves in the bottom of the bilum and carries the infant in it, even when she is working in the garden.

Whether they are working or passing the time of day in talk, the bodies and faces of the highlanders—usually the men—are painted with designs in bright colors. Most of the colors are made from plants and minerals, and some is bought in trade stores. The men and many of the women have had holes drilled through the cartilage that divides the nostrils and some in the soft fleshy flare of the nostrils as well. In these holes they insert a piece of bone or bamboo, pigs' tusks, perhaps a cigarette or a wooden match that someone has given them.

A group of Highlanders in tribal dress watch a modern bridge being built.
Rebecca B. Marcus

But at the time of their *sing-sings*—the ceremonial dances, the women, and more particularly the men, come out in full splendor. Their whole bodies shine with pig grease. They paint designs in brilliant colors over the grease. Flakes of shiny mica, stuck to the grease, glisten in the sun and in the firelight at night. Around their necks, dangling from their ears and across their foreheads they wear many bands and strings of cowry and other shells, dog or pig teeth, and bright feathers. Furry skins of the cuscus, a small wild animal native to New Guinea, hang across their chests and foreheads.

Since much of a man's wealth is measured by his shells the richer ones display big valuable mother-of-pearl crescents around their necks. Curved pig tusks hang down from the holes in their noses, almost to their chins. Their great magnificent headdresses are works of art made of gaily colored feathers and adorned with rows of shells and green scarab beetles. The men of some tribes wear wigs of human hair held in a net, and decorated with feathers and shells. Altogether, the Highlanders' ceremonial dress is probably the most spectacular that can be seen anywhere in the world.

In common with all the people of New Guinea, the Highlanders are divided into tribes. Each tribe in turn is divided into clans and sub-clans. Membership in a clan and sub-clan is counted through the father. Persons in a clan consider themselves brothers or sisters to the others, and so do not marry within their group. They take mates from among other clans in their tribe, or from tribes who are their friends.

There are no chiefs in either a tribe, or a clan, or a village. When a problem arises or a decision is to be made the older men are consulted and their opinion usually accepted.

By tradition, certain tribes are enemies and others friends. Friendly tribes intermarry, exchange gifts, hold feasts together, and call upon each other to help in fighting enemies. It does not take much of an excuse to start a war with an enemy tribe. There may be an argument over a small piece of land, one tribe may accuse the other of woman-stealing, or of having a sorcerer cast a spell on one of its members. There are also wars of revenge for someone killed in an earlier fight.

The men use clubs, bows and arrows, and barbed spears as

weapons. A war seldom lasts more than a day or two. Once blood has been drawn by either side the fighting is usually considered over. There is very little actual killing. The winner is determined by the number of casualties on each side.

As late as the 1940's and 1950's some enemies were captured and eaten. Eating the brains of a wise man was believed to make one wiser, and the flesh of the arm of a strong man made one stronger. To stamp out killing and cannibalism, Australia passed laws to make these practices illegal. Patrol officers and police have been sent in to most areas to enforce the laws, and courts set up to try offenders and sentence them if convicted. Tribal members, however, usually do not reveal who has done the actual killing, and since all the men of a tribe cannot be put in jail, the killer often goes free. As far as the government knows officially, cannibalism has disappeared, but there are rumors that in remote areas it is still practiced. Although warfare has not died out completely, more and more tribesmen are bringing their disputes to courts for settlement.

The people speak many dialects of Motu, a language used by many groups living in the islands of the South Pacific. Because traders and missionaries found it difficult to learn these dialects, they invented a language which they called Pidgin English to communicate with native South Pacific people. It is made up mostly of words based on English with some French, German, and a few local words mixed in. Its spelling and grammar are very simple and the whole language easy to learn. "Sori nogat wok" means, "Sorry we have no work for you;" "Redem gud" means "Read this carefully"; "payback," compensation; and "sing-sing," a traditional ceremony with song and dance. Pidgin English is the common language today between whites and many New Guineans who have learned it.

In their everyday life, the people raise pigs and are small farmers—actually vegetable gardeners. A man clears a piece of ground of trees and brush either with a stone ax or a steel ax that he has obtained by trade, or more usually, by burning off the vegetation. He then apportions the clearing into plots for each of his several wives.

Because the land is mountainous, most of the gardens are on

Highland women twirling fiber into cord. *Rebecca B. Marcus*

steep hillsides. Therefore, unless care is taken the gardens would be
flooded and the soil washed away during the season of heavy rainfall. To prevent this the gardens are terraced and divided into
patches of perhaps twenty feet long and ten or fifteen feet wide.
Each patch is surrounded by a deep drainage ditch to carry off
excess water. The men do most of the work in digging the ditches,
the women help with their four-foot sharp digging sticks, and by
carrying the soil away and spreading it over the plot to be cultivated.
Once a man has fenced in the garden with sharp-pointed stakes to
keep out the pigs, his work is finished. The rest is done by the
women. They plant sweet potatoes, yams, and taro in low mounds
about two feet apart. Sometimes they plant ginger, tobacco, corn,
bananas, or a type of sugar cane. Their only tool is the digging
stick. With it they make holes for planting, cultivate, weed, and dig
up the root crops. Where a crop must be cut they use bamboo knives
or borrow the men's steel axes.

Except for the cuscus and some birds, there are few animals
that can be hunted for food, and these the men shoot with bows and

arrows and the boys with slingshots. Meat is in short supply. Pigs are numerous, but a man's wealth is measured more by the number of pigs he owns than by his shells. Therefore he considers them too valuable to be killed ordinarily for food. When ceremonial dances and celebrations are held his prestige is enhanced by the number of pigs he supplies for the feast. Then the people gorge themselves for days on the roasted meat brought by all the men.

The Highlanders sometimes obtain meat in an unusual way. Just before the dead plants in the garden are to be burned to clear it, the men stretch nets around it, then ignite the dry vegetation. Rats, field mice, and lizards run out of hiding to escape the fire and are caught in the nets. They are then killed, roasted, and eaten.

The food that cannot be eaten raw is wrapped in big leaves and cooked in hot ashes. Some tribes make a kind of oven by digging a three-foot pit in the ground. They put hot rocks in the bottom, then the food wrapped in banana leaves. They place more hot stones over this, then a layer of banana leaves, and seal the pit with dirt. The food, usually sweet potatoes and yams, comes out well-baked and tasty. During feasts, pigs are tied to a rack over an open fire pit and roasted whole. Nowadays some Highlanders buy enamel pots in trade stores and cook their food in them over ashes or small fires.

The Highlanders' tools are simple. Stone ax heads, beautifully polished, are tied with bamboo or other plant fiber to wooden handles. Spears, shields, arrows, clubs and digging sticks are made of wood. Bamboo is used to make knives and the strings of hardwood bows. If they get jobs or sell firewood, crops, stone and shell souvenirs, they earn money to buy simple "store" tools, steel axes and knives, pots, cloth, and matches. If they don't buy matches they can also make fire by sawing a strip of bamboo back and forth under a hardwood stick that rests on a little pile of dried bark. The sparks that are created fall on the grass and ignite it. The men are so skillful in making fire in this way that it seldom takes more than a minute to produce a flame.

Although women supply most of the food, they are not considered as important as men. The men are the masters in the family and in the entire life of the village and tribe.

When a man wants to marry a certain girl and she has consented, he must pay her father and brothers a bride price. The price depends on how strong and healthy she is and how willing to work. If her family thinks it is losing a good worker and provider, it will demand a high price, paid in some cash, but mostly in pigs, stone axes, bird-of-paradise feathers, and cassowaries. The girl's immediate family divides the payment among its male members.

After the bride price has been accepted, the man's family in turn gives gifts, much less lavish, however, to the girl's relatives. A feast of roasted pig provided by both sides follows.

At the time of her betrothal and marriage a girl is decked out magnificently in all the shells, feathers, and cuscus skins her family owns or can borrow. Her skin is greased and her face and breasts brightly painted. Once she joins her husband she returns all this finery and except for an occasional ceremony, becomes a drab, hardworking woman with little time for body ornamentation. Her hands are always busy, in the garden, preparing food, twirling fiber into cord against her thighs, and netting the cord into bilums.

If a girl proves to be an unsatisfactory wife, if she is lazy, quarrelsome, or bears no children, she is sent back to her family and half the bride price must be returned. It is therefore important for her family to try to smooth over any difficulties that may arise between husband and wife.

A rich man may have as many as six wives, for he can pay the bride prices. Most however, can afford only two or three. Each wife has her own hut built for herself and her children by her husband. The hut has a low platform for a bed, perhaps a crude wooden stool or two, and little else. She builds a small fire near the entrance for warmth and for cooking when it rains.

A man spends very little time in the hut of any one wife. He usually sleeps in a men's house, a sort of clubhouse, more comfortable than the women's huts. Its roof is higher, it is airier, and less smoky. Sleeping platforms line most of its two long sides. Here all the men congregate, discuss whatever plans or business they have, and hold secret religious practices. At the age of about eight, or in some tribes after special initiation ceremonies, a boy leaves his mother's hut to sleep in the men's house. Women and girls are forbidden ever to enter.

A Highlander wearing a decorated wig of human hair. *Letitia B. Scott*

The New Guinea people do not believe in gods or in any supernatural being. Instead, they believe that the spirits of their ancestors are with them, to help or harm them. The men perform rituals to control and guide these spirits. In some tribes they wear wooden masks, paint their bodies specially, and dance to the beating of drums and the blowing of sacred flutes.

Among the Highlanders there are tribes that set the body of a dead man in a sitting position on a platform in the village for all to see. The body is kept there until the flesh is gone, then the skull is removed and the rest of the bones buried. The skull is kept, with others, on a ceremonial platform in the village. Most tribes also preserve the skulls of their ancestors and keep them in the men's houses. Some paint the skulls; others fill them out with clay and then paint over this to give a lifelike appearance.

Before boys are permitted to join in any of these rituals they must undergo painful and frightening initiation ceremonies. Several boys of the tribe, between the ages of 13 and 16, are initiated at the same time. They are kept together, away from the girls and women. At some time during the ceremony incisions are made in parts of their bodies until blood flows freely. The tribesmen say that the boy is being freed of his mother's blood in this way, and now is a complete male. He is taught the secret rituals and admitted to adulthood.

In many tribes, when a man dies his close relatives cover their chests and faces with gray clay as a sign of mourning. The women of his family not only plaster themselves with clay but wear a great many strings of small gray seeds, called Job's tears. There are frequently so many of these strings of Job's tears that they cover the shoulders and torso to the waist like a cape. Until recently, close relatives cut off a finger at the first joint as a special sign of mourning, but this practice has been abandoned.

Belief in witchcraft and sorcery play a large part in the lives of the New Guinea people. Each village has at least one witch or sorcerer who, the people believe, can cure illness by using secret magical chants and charms. The sorcerer is also thought to cause disease, death, crop failure, or other disaster to an enemy tribe. This has led to many tribal wars in the past, and sometimes still does.

A widow in mourning, her face painted with clay and torso covered with strings of Job's tears. *Rebecca B. Marcus*

But the belief in magic as the cause of disease is weakening, as the Australian government sets up more and more health centers. Now it is not uncommon for a sick person to be brought to a center for treatment, even though suspicion of the white man's medicine still lingers. Some women even go to a center's small hospital to give birth to their babies. If, in spite of medical treatment, it is obvious that a patient is about to die, the people of his village carry him back on a litter so that he may die among his family and friends.

The government has done much more for Papua-New Guinea than establishing health centers. Under the trusteeship of the United Nations, it is working to unite the many warring tribes into one nation, able to govern itself. The first and most important step in this direction is the establishment of more schools so that a greater number of children will be able to attend.

There are now central schools in many parts of the territory. Most of the teachers are native New Guineans trained either in Australia or in one of the several teachers' colleges in Papua-New Guinea. The language used is English, but the teachers also speak the native Motu dialect. Some schools have living quarters for those children whose homes are far away, but pupils usually walk several miles each way to and from school.

A father enrolls a boy in school hoping the child will learn enough to get a job in town and bring money back to the village. Very few girls go to school, since the bride price they bring the family depends on how well they work in the gardens and at home.

There are other kinds of education offered to make the people ready for independence. Livestock experts have brought in cows and chickens and taught the people how to raise them. Agriculture officers have introduced new vegetables so that the people's diet will be more varied and nutritious.

Some years ago white Australians established coffee plantations in the Highlands. Many black New Guineans now own coffee groves either privately or as cooperatives. Tea, too, has been planted, although not as extensively as coffee. Sometimes the money earned from the sale of these crops goes to buy western-type goods and machinery for a village—a small truck, a station wagon, or a small tractor. Individuals buy steel knives and axes, matches, cigarettes, soft drinks, and sometimes a transistor radio. Some of the money is used to send a boy to high school and perhaps college.

It is also used to buy cowrie and mother-of-pearl shells, bird-of-paradise feathers, and paint for their bodies. It is saved up to pay a bride price, or as compensation in a tribal payback.

September 16 of each year is National Independence Day for all of Papua-New Guinea. Tribesmen from every part of the country come in full ceremonial dress by plane, truck, or bus to Port

Moresby, the capital, and to other big towns that have sprung up in the country. Friend and enemy join in celebrating this day of unity and future independence, to show their tribal dances and engage in competitive sports. The government of the country hopes that in this way the different tribes will get to know each other and discover that it is better to be friends than enemies.

Papua-New Guinea became self-governing in December, 1973, and is due to become fully independent in 1975 or 1976. It has a prime minister and a parliament, to which tribes elect representatives. A legislative council was elected in 1964 for the first time, in preparation for self-government. For this election, Australian government patrol officers went into towns and villages to explain what "election" and "legislative assembly" mean. They used loudspeakers, tape recorders, and filmstrips, to the wonder of many of the people who had never imagined such things existed.

Enemy tribes agreed to a one-month truce to allow safe, free movement to the voting places. The ballots were cards with pictures of the candidates, for most of the people cannot read.

The new legislative assembly has set up some of its own courts to settle disputes over such things as land and pig ownership. Questions that do not arise in our culture are sometimes brought to a court for a decision. One such concerned a bride price. A group of young men banded together and claimed they could not get married because the bride price had become too high. The judge considered the question and handed down this decision: A new bride is worth five pigs, one cassowary, and the equivalent of 300 Australian dollars. A woman married once before may fetch two pigs, one cassawary, and $37.50, but a woman married more than once has no commercial value.

Australia does not plan to abandon Papua-New Guinea completely when it becomes independent. It will keep many of its experts there, and grant large sums of money to help the new country develop. Perhaps present tribal life will become less important to the people as time goes on, and become even more a mixture of both native and western cultures.

9

An Amazon Tribe Takes Its First
Step Toward the Outside World
The Kranhacãrores of Brazil

DEEP IN THE Amazon jungle of Brazil lives a tribe of Indians, the Kranhacãrores, who until February, 1973 had never met anyone outside their tribe except a few other Indians. They heard from others that there are people whose skins are light, almost white, and from the cover of the jungle, had even seen some of them. But always, they abandoned their village and retreated further into the forest when they thought the white men were making camp too close by.

The Kranhacãrores are suspicious of all strangers, and especially fearful of intrusion by white men into their hunting grounds. They have heard tales of how white men had come into Indian lands, killed many of their people, driven out the rest, and taken away the land. This they were determined to prevent.

But the Brazilian government is building a road through the jungle to promote mining and prospecting for gemstones, and a section of this road is to go through some of the Kranhacãrore hunting grounds. In the past, the road planners had taken what land they wanted without much thought for the people living on it. The Indians, enraged, turned about and raided the camps of the builders, killing some of the workers.

Now the government thought it best to pave the way to peaceful relations by sending in government agents first to make contact with the Indians in remote areas. These agents hoped to gain the confidence of the Indians, assure them that only a very small part of their land would be taken, and the rest left for them. Their hunting grounds would barely be touched, and the people themselves would not be harmed in any way. In fact, they would profit by receiving modern tools, utensils, and medical aid. The National Indian Foundation of Brazil, FUNAI, was given this task, and the brothers Claudio and Orlando Villas Boas, placed in charge.

The Villas Boas brothers were directors of the Xingu preserve, an area set aside for Indians in the Amazon jungle. In questioning Indians in the Xingu about other tribes, they learned that there was one, the Kranhacãrores, a group of fierce jungle dwellers. It was rumored that they killed any outsider they meet, because they trust no one who is not of their own tribe.

The answers to further questions gave them some idea of where to look for this tribe. In January, 1972, from a helicopter, Claudio Villas Boas scanned the area and saw smoke and what appeared to be huts in a small clearing. He returned to the Xingu preserve, and induced a few of the Indians to act as guides to bring him close to the Kranhacãrores.

The Indian guides scouted the jungle and sure enough, found traces that people were living near where the smoke had been seen. One clue was the skull of a monkey that had been shot with an arrow no more than three days earlier. Villas Boas thought, therefore, that this would be a good place to start to make contact with the hidden tribe. He had a small airstrip built, and set up camp along a nearby stream.

To show they had come in peace, the government agent strung up lines across a trail a short distance from his camp, and hung up presents of pots, plastic basins, and steel axes and knives. Days passed, but nothing happened, and then, one morning, the knives and axes were gone.

For months, he kept on leaving presents tied to the lines. Usually, during the night, all but the plastic objects were taken, but there was no other sign of the Indians. At last, one day the guides saw three Kranhacãrores standing silently on the bank across the stream, watching the camp. They were taller than most Indians, but like men of other jungle tribes, dressed only in loin cloths. The guides spoke to them, gave them bird calls, but got no answer. As silently as they had stood watching, the three men disappeared into the forest. They had come, Villas Boas decided, to see for themselves what these strange men were like.

Villas Boas continued his patient wait, and time and time again the Kranhacãrores let themselves be glimpsed for just a few minutes, then melted into the jungle. Some days the agent saw no smoke at all in the distance, showing that the Indians had moved away, only to come back a week or so later.

Boldly, Villas Boas and his guides finally went to the place where they had seen smoke rising only the day before. They found a group of rude shelters made of poles, with leaf-covered roofs, but there were no people. Fresh banana peels showed that the village had just been abandoned. The Kranhacãrores were evidently frightened by the approach of the strangers and had gone off hurriedly, because they had left behind some of the steel and stone axes they needed to make their new shelters.

The intruders left more gifts of pots, beads, and mirrors in the village. They came back the next day, and found that everything but the mirrors and the plastic pots had been taken. The Indians had smashed the mirrors, perhaps afraid the reflecting glass might be a kind of strange magic. But, where the gifts had been, the Kranhacãrores had put presents of wooden clubs in return. It seemed they finally wanted to make a gesture of friendship. But nevertheless, Villas Boas decided to move slowly to allay any fears the Kranhacãrores might still have, and waited for them to make the next move.

A year after he had first set up his camp, Villas Boas' scouts informed him that the Indians were planning some action. They had seen the tribesmen gathered in the jungle a short distance away, holding council. About two weeks later, his year-long patience was rewarded. Twenty men of the tribe timidly came out to greet the white men. The Kranhacãrores had taken their first step toward the outside world.

The Indian who appeared to be the chief embraced Villas Boas as a sign of good will, then brought out presents of bows, arrows, and wooden clubs. The white man returned the embrace, and offered him more of the things he had been leaving for the Indians. However, he did not give him anything made of plastic, because, in the past, they had never taken a plastic object. Few words were spoken, for neither knew the language of the other, but words were not needed. Good relations had been established.

The Kranhacãrores took Villas Boas and his party to their village. He found, as he had thought, that they are Stone Age people who had no iron tools except those given them by the white men. They have never learned to make clay pots, build canoes to ride the jungle rivers, or grind manioc roots into flour as most South American Indians do. They weave palm leaves into baskets in which they keep fruits, roots, and berries that they gather.

The wild banana is their most abundant food. When they strip one clump of trees of the ripe fruit, they break camp, move close to another wild banana plantation, and build new huts. They use clubs and bows and arrows to hunt monkeys and small animals, and catch fish in nets woven from vines.

Very little is known about their family life, customs, or religion. The Villas-Boas brothers might have learned more, but they have left FUNAI because they disagreed with its policy. They think the agency is more interested in opening the vast Amazon lands to settlers and prospectors than in protecting the Indians. FUNAI's main purpose, they claim, is to pacify the Indians so that they will be less hostile to those encroaching on their grounds.

The Villas-Boas brothers may very well be right. True, FUNAI agents have given the Kranhacãrores some iron tools, pots, and clothing. But they have also given them a taste for food and other things they did not have in their old hunting days and no means to satisfy these tastes. Many have taken to the roadsides to beg for a few coins, some food, matches, and cigarettes they never needed before.

However, the Kranhacãrores are getting help from another Indian tribe, the Xavantes. This tribe has been in contact with white men for some time, and has learned to adapt more to the change in their lives. They are showing the Kranhacãrores better techniques in fishing and preparing foods, and some hygiene and health care. But mainly, the Xavantes say, they want to ally themselves with the Kranhacárores to try to keep white men from robbing both of all their lands.

There may indeed come a time when most of the Indian tribes of the Amazon will band together to fight for the land they consider rightfully theirs.

A young Kranhacárore tribesman. *Wide World Photos*

Bibliography

GENERAL

Brain, Robert. *Into The Primitive Environment*. Prentice-Hall, Inc., Englewood Cliffs, New Jersey. 1972.
Cotlow, Lewis. *The Twilight of the Primitive*. Macmillan Company, New York. 1971.
National Geographic. Vanishing Peoples of the Earth. National Geographic Special Publications Division, Washington, D. C. 1968.
Ottenberg, Simon and Phoebe, eds. *Cultures and Societies of Africa*. Random House, New York. 1960.
Pinney, Roy. *Vanishing Tribes*. T. Y. Crowell, New York. 1968.
Skinner, Elliott P., ed. *Peoples and Cultures of Africa*. Doubleday–Natural History Press, Garden City, N. Y. 1973.
Weyer, Edward. *Primitive People Today*. Doubleday Co., Garden City, N. Y. 1959.

KRANHACÃRORES

Indigena. News from Indian America. 1973, 1974. *Brazilian Indian Policy*. 1973. P. O. Box 4073, Berkeley, Calif.
The New York Times. February 11, 1973; November 9, 1974.
Saturday Review of the Sciences. April, 1973, Vol. 1, No. 3, p. 82. Saturday Review Industries, New York.
The Tribe That Hides From Man. Television film produced by Adrian Cowell, ATV Management Services, Ltd., London. 1972.
Villas-Boas, Claudio and Orlando. *Xingu*. Farrar, Straus and Giroux, New York. 1973.

JIVARO

Harner, Michael J. *The Jivaro*. Doubleday Co., Garden City, N. Y. 1973.
Indigena. News From Indian America. 1974. P. O. Box 4073, Berkeley, Calif.

PYGMIES

Turnbull, Colin M. *The Forest People*. Simon and Schuster, New York. 1968.

BUSHMEN

Thomas, Elizabeth M. *The Harmless People*. Alfred A. Knopf, New York. 1959.
Turnbull, Colin M. *The People of Africa*. World Publishing Company, New York. 1962.
Van der Post, Laurens. *The Heart of the Hunter*. Wm. Morrow, New York. 1971.

IK

Turnbull, Colin M. *The Mountain People*. Simon and Schuster, New York. 1973.

JUNGLE NEGRITOS

Cipriani, Lidio. *The Andaman Islanders*. F. A. Praeger, New York. 1966.
Radcliffe-Browne, Alfred R. *The Andaman Islanders*. Free Press–Macmillan, New York. 1964 edition.

TASADAY

"Cave People of the Philippines." NBC broadcast and script, Oct. 6, 1972.
The New York Times. October 8, 1972; December 23, 1973.

AUSTRALIAN ABORIGINALS

Australian Consulate Information Service, New York. Press releases and pamphlets of Australian Government Department of Aboriginal Affairs. November 11, 1973; November 23, 1973; media releases for July, 1974.
Baker, Eleanor Z. *The Australian Aborigines*. Steck-Vaughn Co., Texas. 1968.
Berndt, Ronald M. and Catherine H. *The World of the First Australians*. Ure Smith, Ltd. Sydney, Australia. 1964.
Elkin, A. P. *The Australian Aborigines*. Angus and Robertson, Sydney, Australia. 1968.
Gould, Richard A. *Yawara*. Charles Scribner's, New York. 1971.
Indriess, Ion L. *Our Living Stone Age*. Angus and Robertson, Sydney, Australia. 1963.
Identity: Journal of Opinion. Aboriginal Publications Foundation, Perth, Australia. July, 1974; October, 1974; January, 1975.
The New York Times. November 25, 1973.

NEW GUINEA

Read, Kenneth. *The High Valley*. Charles Scribner's Sons, New York. 1965.
Rowley, C. D. *The New Guinea Villager*. F. W. Cheshire, Melbourne, Australia. 1964.
Salisbury, R. F. *From Stone to Steel*. Melbourne University Press, Melbourne, Australia. 1962.
Simpson, Colin. *Plumes and Arrows*. Angus and Robertson, Sydney, Australia. 1962.
Sinclair, James. *The Highlanders*. Jacaranda Press, Ltd., Brisbane, Australia. 1971.
Sinclair, James. *Faces of New Guinea*. Jacaranda Press, Ltd., Brisbane, Australia. 1975.
The New York Times. February 3, 1974.
Williams, Maslyn. *The Stone Age Island*. Doubleday Co., Garden City, N. Y. 1964.

Index